THE CHRISTIAN IMPRINT

THE CHRISTIAN IMPRINT

Fred Pierce Corson

ABINGDON PRESS

NEW YORK   •   NASHVILLE

THE CHRISTIAN IMPRINT

Copyright MCMLV by Pierce & Washabaugh

Library of Congress Catalog Card Number: 55-6761

SET UP, PRINTED, AND BOUND BY THE PARTHENON PRESS, AT NASHVILLE, TENNESSEE, UNITED STATES OF AMERICA

1149397

THIS IS FOR

LINDA ELLEN and her generation

FOREWORD

We have been living long enough in this turbulent and destructive era to realize that the condition is not superficial nor incidental. Its causes and effects go deep into life. To get at the heart of our trouble and to apply a cure, we must look seriously at ourselves. What we are and what we do fashion what we become. Until we recognize the spiritual nature of the ills which plague our century, there can be little permanent improvement expected. Their source and their correction lie within.

Palliatives for our afflictions have been generously applied and have proven very costly. It would seem that money is no object in what the world has been trying to do for the restoration of its health. But all these quick cures and external remedies have done no more than to bring a temporary relief. They have worked for a soothing effect on the inflammation. They have not removed the causes.

This book is an attempt to lift up the sources as well as the occasions of our present difficulties and to direct our thought to the real nature of the disease and to a remedy which will cure.

The remedy offered is the Christian way of life, applied, developed, and maintained through education.

The confusion of this generation about itself and its hesitancy to face the moral and spiritual demands for its recovery indicate the extremity of its plight. Something which will stimulate the rank and file to right action must work soon and fast or be too late.

It is hoped, therefore, that the discussion which follows will not only alert the readers to the emergency which is upon us but also quicken and expand the efforts to cure this twentieth-century sickness.

Because so many must be involved in producing an improvement in our life and world, I have endeavored to keep the non-specialist in mind and to avoid as far as possible technical language in the presentation of the theme. Creating better people who in turn will make a better world is everybody's business.

The content of these chapters was presented as the Quillian Lectures at the Candler School of Theology, Emory University. Their reception by the students, faculty, and visitors confirmed my belief that there is a wide current of interest in character education and a waiting response for a positive program of Christian improvement. Henry B. Trimble, then dean of the Candler School, as always was the soul of courtesy; and his suggestions regarding both the theme and its presentation reflected the close relation he has always maintained with the people whom his students ultimately serve.

Appreciation is expressed to many who directly and indirectly contributed in the preparation of the manuscript and to my secretary, Miss Florence M. Waer, who typed these pages and verified the references. I am greatly indebted to Dr. John D. Herr for his painstaking work on the index.

For all who have a love for youth I feel a deep kinship, and the many evidences of their eager desire to know what to do with their young have prompted me to make available my experience in this field as a minister, educator, and father.

FRED PIERCE CORSON

CONTENTS

———

9

CHAPTER I

WHOSE IMAGE?

*And Jesus said to them, "Whose likeness
and inscription is this?"*—MATT. 22:20

*The life of a man . . . in God must bear the
stamp of Christ.*—I JOHN 1 (Phillips)

THE CONTROLS OF THE FUTURE ARE THE CONCERN OF THE
present. What is done today puts its imprint upon the life of
tomorrow. Each day or each era is not a clean sheet inserted in
the book of life without connection with what has gone before
or is to follow. Life is not a loose-leaf notebook to which we add
or remove at will. Life is a bound volume, all of one piece, with
each page a unit in the continued story.

What produces the pages which unfold the story of life is
a question of great importance. We develop the controls for
the future in the light of what we believe determines the future.
Some think that geography plots the story in the book of life.
They hold the belief that environment is the deciding factor in
shaping the future. Atmosphere and climate, the nature of the
terrain, the availability of natural resources, sanitation, and
social qualifications are the cards from which these predictors
make their prophecies of things to come. While none would
discount the significance of these environmental factors, many
would question whether they are the cause of a type of life
or its effect, whether they produce life or life models them.

11

And to accept this theory as the sole control of the future leaves us with too many unanswered questions and unexplained situations. Experience teaches that the good life is not the inevitable result of fortuitous circumstances.

Others hold that the economic yardstick is the measure of the future. What happens in tomorrow's world, they say, will be the result of the production and distribution of the goods to live with. So they argue about the merits of the various economic systems for insuring an abundant life to come on the basis that the more one has the better he will be, until when everybody has everything, the utopia will have actually arrived. This theory of the haves and the have-nots has been used to justify wars and to excuse the social evils and the personal derelictions of our age. It offers, however, a questionable explanation for the multiple violation of the Commandments of God, especially the Eighth Commandment, which says, "Thou shalt not steal." It has no explanation whatever for the haves who violate the Tenth Commandment ("Thou shalt not covet") and the modern Ahabs who, possessing everything, still are not satisfied until, like their ancient prototype, they take also poor Naboth's vineyard. Nor does this theory of the good life through the just distribution of material things assure the elimination of sins such as David committed against Uriah.

Others see the next chapters in the book of life written by the hand of science. Invention is the mother of the future, they say. So they wait breathlessly for each new gadget which science turns out for the convenience of man. It is, to be sure, an irrefutable conclusion that the more man discovers, the greater will his life be changed. But whether the changes will be for better or for worse, science gives no assurance because it cannot guarantee the decisions of man in handling scientific power. What man does with his knowledge colors the future, and the use of knowledge requires both moral and emotional judgments.

Others see politics exercising control over the future and etching the lines in the face of things to come. The good life, they say, is the product of the mechanics of control; and government expanded to world proportions is the medium through which these processes, which control society, can be exercised. As a method we agree with this position. But before we can predict their effect upon our lives, we must make two other fundamental decisions: first, how are the mechanics of government to be created; and second, who will operate them?

Now the Christian answer to these questions raised by the popular theories for the control of the future is personality. Christianity puts man at the controls of life. The other theories are the corollaries to the main proposition and must make their contribution or work their destruction through the direction of the people who operate them.

According to the Christian position the key to the future is the people who will live in it, and any consideration of what the future will be must take into account the manner of persons we ought to become who expect to hasten the day of the Lord (II Peter 3:11). People are the deciding factors in shaping the things to come. They are the cause for what happens rather than its effect. Thus people are not the little and insignificant element in a vast and powerful universe as some have depicted them. People are the powerful and deciding element in a universe created for their use. This point of view offers the Christian faith the leading role in creating a "new earth in which righteousness dwells" by developing people who will not be judged unworthy to possess that better day.

How to create the people, who are required for the accomplishment of the plan of God for the world, is the task of Christian education, applied in its widest application to all phases and ages of life and achieved through all the avenues by which people acquire the knowledge and skills for living.

THE MATERIAL

When we think of the Christian plan to prepare for tomorrow's world, we are reminded at once of the presence and importance of youth. They are the material out of which the future will be made, and they must constitute the starting point in developing the good life. A newspaper editorial reminded a generation smug with its materialism and deluded by its scientific power that the children of today are the hope and the assurance of the future. It said:

Your boy is the person who is going to carry on what you have started. He is to sit where you are sitting and attend to those things which you think are so important when you are gone. You may adopt all the policies you please, but how they are to be carried out depends on him. Even if you make leagues and treaties, he will have to manage them. He is going to sit at your desk in the Senate and occupy your place on the Supreme Bench. He will assume control of your cities, states and nations. He is going to move in and take over your prisons, churches, schools, universities and corporations. All your work is going to be judged and praised or condemned by him. Your reputation and your fortune are in his hands. All your work is for him and the fate of the nations and of humanity is likewise in his hands. So it might be well to pay him some attention.[1]

This editorial reflects the judgment of the wise in every generation. Plato called youth a "time when character is molded and easily takes the impress one may wish to stamp upon it."

Jesus in a world which rated importance in terms of adulthood made children the object of his special attention.

John Dickinson, colonial governor of Pennsylvania, at a time when the institutions of the New Republic were taking shape, warned of the tragic failure which would result if "we provide them [the younger generation] with an economic competence and deny them the education to use it properly."

---

[1] Used by permission of the *San Francisco Examiner*.

14

We who believe the plan of God for the world is actual and possible ignore these challenges to a Christian-directed education for our children at the peril of failure. The Christian goal must be clearly seen, and everything that touches life must be judged in the light of the contribution it makes toward the achievement of the goal. Does it advance or hinder, destroy or build, hurt or help?

The advocates of undirected education, who make no selection of the influences which are molding the life of their children on the theory that it is educationally unscientific to do so, should restudy their position in the light of the results. No theory has the right to exist unless it earns it by what it achieves when applied to life. And we have had ample evidence of the untrustworthiness of a popular secularistic theory of education which leaves selection too much in the hands of the immature and the incompetent. Plato put a question to our generation as well as his own when he asked, "Shall we simply allow our children to listen to any stories that one happens to make up, and so receive into their minds ideas often the very opposite to those we think they ought to have when they grow up?"

If youth is to live the good life and make a good world, the question of "whose likeness and inscription" he shall bear becomes a matter of first and supreme importance. The influences which surround the young leave their mark upon their adult life. We owe it to youth to see that these influences are both good and adequate. They should touch all phases of their life for the better. And the facts will not warrant the assumption that in home, school, community, and church we have provided a set of educative influences which will assure a future in keeping with the plan of God for the world. Clear thinking, based upon a sincere facing of the facts, constitutes the immediate challenge in the situation which confronts us. Bold speaking in behalf of Christian conclusions and colossal planning to put them into effect must follow if tomorrow's men and tomorrow's world are to be better.

Certainly in a world where so much awaits a new generation for its improvement, we would do well to follow Jesus' example and set this generation of youth in our midst in order that we might see our young in the light of what we expect them to do.

Such an examination of the material out of which tomorrow's world will be built is both disturbing and hopeful. It reveals a quantity and quality to work with and an unjustifiable negligence in what is being done with the material. There are about 62,000,000 young people in the United States at the present time, and their number increases by about 4,000,000 each year. All the mentally competent among them over five years of age are in schools for secular education five days a week. That is good. But for religious instruction only 35,000,000 of them are in our church schools one hour on an average of every other week. And 60 per cent of those who are in church schools at ten years of age will be out at sixteen years of age. Twenty-five million of them have no connection whatever with any religious training. Of this 25,000,000, who from the Christian standpoint are unschooled and uneducated, the Protestant churches have a normal responsibility for 60 per cent or about 15,000,000.

These figures, which we can fully comprehend only when we lift up the younger generation and look at them as a unit, present a formidable task to the forces who would put upon our young the Christian imprint. However, this task, with the available resources and favorable circumstances at our command, is small when compared to the task of putting that imprint upon the youth around the world. But if we are to take the kingdoms of this world and make them Christ's, we must first take the kingdom's children and make them Christian. And this is an undertaking which faces fierce and well-organized opposition. There is not universal acceptance of the plan of God for the life of men and for the world they live in. Allowing for honest doubt on the part of some, we still must face the fact that strong and effective forces are at work in the world to destroy the plan of God and to remove the Christian imprint from life. The task of Christianizing life is not simply a matter of interest and activity. It involves a struggle "against the principalities, against the powers, against the world rulers of this present darkness, against the spiritual hosts of wickedness in the heavenly places" (Eph. 6:12), a new Lucifer brilliant and powerful leading a rebellion on earth against the rule from heaven.

What our children shall become, whose men they shall be, if the Christian answer is to prevail, can no longer await the leisurely and secondary consideration which has constituted the Christian strategy in the past.

THE STRUGGLE FOR POSSESSION

The struggle for the possession of our young is now on. The issue is clearly drawn. The question raised about the control of the coin symbolizes the determining factor in the possession of our youth. Whether they shall be Christ's or Caesar's, the children of darkness or the children of light, followers of God or slaves to Mammon, depends, as Jesus pointed out in regard to the coin, on whose imprint they bear.

The answer is found in the imprint. The trade-mark identifies the claim. Whose they are and whose they will become are not established either by our desire or by our proclamations or by our legal decisions. The mold used in their minting determines what they shall be like and in whose service they shall circulate.

The New Testament imagery which I have used throughout must not be taken to imply that life is wooden and that the educational process is mechanical. Character is the result of the person's creative response to all the influences which play upon his life, as I shall develop particularly in Chapter V. Neverthe-

17

less, it is not wise to pretend to an objectivity we cannot achieve. The lives of those engaged in learning *are* influenced, shaped, molded, by the ideals and values of those who are their teachers. We do clearly bear the imprint of one set of values or another, and Christian education need not apologize for making explicit the Christian presuppositions on which it operates. It is this aspect of the educational process which needs a fresh consideration in an age when Christianity's competitors have discovered its power and are using it for their evil designs.

Christianity does not have the field to itself in molding youth. There are competitors who are aggressive and clever. They have taken advantage of Christianity's antiquated methods and inactivity until they have established exclusive rights in molding more than one third of the world's youth and challenged Christianity's priority with the other two thirds.

The Christian way can no longer assume that its superiority and acceptance go without question. They are questioned and superseded on every hand. Christianity, if it is to increase its output of Christlike people, must understand the nature of its competition and develop the methods required to deal with it.

The competitors of Christianity in the development of personality can be separated into three groups. They are at work in every community and in all the institutions of community life. They operate both openly and by indirection. And they are out to take over the business of conditioning our youth for their life as adults. The Christian forces must know everything there is to know about these competitors if they are to win over them.

The secularists constitute one of these groups. They are the people who create and operate the influences at work in the world which encourage man to ignore God. They look on Christian morality as a trifle. They consider religion as incidental, and they think of God as of little or no account. In their scheme God has no priorities. He exists, but he does not rule. They believe that man and not God issues the commands for living. Like the Corinthians of the first century "they unfortunately have no awareness of God" (I Cor. 15:34).[2]

The secularists are the most difficult competitors with which Christianity must deal because they permeate and do not localize. They are not confined to one place, nor are they evident in any particular phase of life. Secularism is an attitude which gets into everything that a person does. Its distinguishing marks are often disguised by a normalcy which makes them difficult to identify. Secularism is at home in religion. It will be found lifting its voice in religious sentimentality and in observing the forms of religious ceremonialism. It is active in good works, advocating the by-products of Christianity such as honesty, charity, brotherhood, and service and offering the humanism of self-interest as a substitute for life's values which Christianity acknowledges because they have their origin and validation in God.

These secularistic forces have honeycombed our education both public and religious. In the case of public education they have pushed God out by making it illegal to offer him as a subject or to include him as an activity. At best he now stands on the periphery of public education without priority or equality in relation to the subjects considered essential to develop an understanding of life's major values. Whatever may be the present legal justification for the nonrecognition of the spiritual as a part of the educational responsibility in training the young, the results of it are proving disastrous to our way of life. It is becoming increasingly apparent that if children are educated in a pattern of life which has no place for a consideration of God as supreme and final, barring a miracle, the outcome will be a generation of pagans. They may be nice, well-mannered, sophisticated, intelligent, and efficient pagans; but at the places of decision they are pagans.

This same spirit of secularism has had its influence also on

---

[2] Wand, *New Testament Letters* (Oxford University Press).

religious education in the ensmallment of God's person and his place in human life. The very attitude, which in most communities goes unchallenged, that an hour a week, when one feels like it, is sufficient for the purposes of religious education entrenches the prevailing impression that God is something less than all important. Add to this an instructional conception of God which portrays him as a humanistic force promoting good works, but not as a spiritual personality in fellowship with human life; and secularism gains an ally in the Church for its campaign to make God an elective rather than a requirement.

The Christian pattern in education on all levels also faces serious competition from the atheists, who condition modern society to deny God. The new atheism with which this generation must deal is different from the earlier intellectual variety which was limited by an eclectic clientele and by an unpopular and impractical appeal. The atheism which denies the existence of God on solely intellectual grounds is not difficult to deal with. It claims less than one per cent of the population in the United States. It is not increasing in numbers because the atmosphere is not right for the spread and growth of its kind. "In the light of present world conditions," as Dwight D. Eisenhower once said, "only a stupid person can be an intellectual atheist."

The denial of God, however, recruits its adherents today for a pattern of conduct which expresses itself in a political crusade. Mighty forces are at work in the world to destroy people's belief in God for purposes of political domination and exploitation. They attack God not to destroy him as their final objective, but by destroying man's spiritual defenses they aim ultimately for the destruction of human freedom. This freedom, which is basic to all other freedom, is fought for, won, and kept by spiritual resources. In dealing with people around us we cannot surrender a place for the spiritual nurture of life without destroying the kind of freedom which makes our way of life possible. An easy tolerance for a vocal God-denying minority is the sure way to spiritual self-destruction. Freedom in the Christian meaning of that word depends upon spiritual worth for its value and spiritual power for its cultivation and defense.

Whether it is a form of Fascism, which seeks to destroy faith in God by ignoring him in the ways of daily living, or a form of Communism, which would soul-wash the individual by incessant activities which deny God's existence, the result is the same. By it man loses his sense of dignity, importance, and responsibility. He surrenders his fundamental rights. He sinks to a lower status of creation. In the eyes of those who rule he becomes a commodity, a pawn, and a slave.

Sometimes those who raise their voices against these non-theistic or antitheistic forces at work in all phases of modern society are discounted by a label which in fact is a libel. They are shouted down as witch-hunters, and the term is indiscriminately used by both the extreme right and the extreme left. The menace of the catchword, the slogan, the unanalyzed phrase "for whose currency men of fame are often responsible," is a serious threat both to Christianity and to democracy.

However, those who are committed to the goal of Christian personality and understand its methods of achievement cannot afford to be too sensitive to the phrase-making proclivities of their opponents. The master Teacher was the object of name calling, but he never permitted the labels men gave him to confuse the argument or becloud the issue. He was never distracted by them, nor did he shrink from the unpopularity which resulted when he spoke up for the things he believed in. The issue was greater to him than his sensitive feelings. Perhaps if the older generation thought less of current social ostracism and more of the future opinion of the young, when maturity gives them a more accurate sense of the values of life, a better job of personality development for both young and old would result.

A much more practical strategy is also necessary if these influences defacing the Christian imprint upon personality are to be removed. They cannot be dealt with effectively in a detached and academic manner. Conferences and resolutions do not deter them so long as down-to-earth application of the conclusions to specific situations do not follow. A statement of beliefs is innocuous provided the proclaimers of it do nothing to stop the removal of the landmarks of religion from personal and corporate living. While Christianity is content to be a voice crying in the wilderness, "Prepare the way of the Lord" (Isa. 40:3), these forces take their antireligious campaigns to the places where people live. They deal in their conferences with such questions as "how to protect youth from the influences of religion" (a theme used in an East Germany Youth Conference). They do not confine their discussions to the leadership group as Christianity so often does. They take their message to the common man through an evangelism which they call propaganda. Typical of what they do is the report of the Department of Antireligious Propaganda for the year 1952 in Bulgaria, a nation of seven million people, where in one year under official guidance 90,000 lectures on atheism were given and 1,600,000 adherents reported.

Christianity often allows these groups under the guise of liberal patriotism to put its people on the defensive. They talk big about human rights, but without a word concerning the right of a person to know God and to serve him. They extol man's duty to the state and are silent on man's higher duty to the power which created both him and the state. They treat religion as the interloper, and defending its position rather than attacking theirs has given Christianity a disadvantage in a consideration of its place and claims.

A third group of Christianity's competitors constitute the most formidable menace to the Christian imprint in the United States. They may be called the "Iniquitous," who condition people to defy God. They challenge the authority of God in

22

human life. They do not attack his existence; rather they acknowledge his reality but refute his wisdom. They have in fact removed him from office. He no longer holds the position of lawgiver and judge. For the word of God, which Christians believe "standeth sure," they offer a moral relativism which proceeds on the assumption that in this world it is every man for himself in the field of moral decisions and that the rules can be altered at will to suit the players.

They offer man a new measure for the soundness and adequacy of his decisions. He no longer needs to bother himself with the question "Is it right?" His only concern now is with the question "Does it pay?" Thus they commercialize everything that has to do with life by making profit its justification. Moral considerations, social responsibility, and personal welfare are voted down by the overruling motive of "What is there in it for me?"

The extent to which this group controls life in these United States can be measured by the infiltration of this spirit into all lines of activity. Public amusement, literature, and personal services from the cradle to the grave, even religion, show the influences of this policy widely accepted which creates false and artificial needs and gives the people whatever they will pay for. Such influences are, in fact, the economic termites eating away the foundations of sound business; and if another economic crash should come to the United States, they will be the underlying cause of it.

Then this group has gone about making sin respectable. They have performed a face-lifting operation on vice and glamorized wrongdoing. Venetian blinds, soft lights, men of distinction, the mannerisms of sophistication, are the props used to create this gigantic deception. Sin has been made prevalent and easy. Endorsements to ease the conscience of the religious and sensible have been abundantly available for a consideration. Values are now being determined by entertainment appeal. Acceptance for the questionable is being gained through the medium of familiarity.

The strength and danger of this element in contemporary life lie in its acceptance by a generation which has become accustomed to its presence. Modern purveyors of vice know that

> Vice is a monster of so frightful mien,
> As to be hated needs but to be seen.

But they also know the tendency of human nature to accommodate itself to its surroundings, so the vice of the twentieth century no longer scandalizes because in this generation,

> Yet seen too oft, familiar with her face,
> We first endure, then pity, then embrace.

The new status of gambling and liquor is a clear indication of how familiarity can change public opinion in the brief span of a generation. A voice of religion now pleads without a blush for legalized gambling, and no one seems shocked at the fact that in these United States there are more barmaids than college girls. The difficulties in dealing with this God-defying challenge to the Christian pattern are increased by a spirit, not only of rebellion against God's control of life, but also of an open denial of its validity. The strategy used against it in the past is not proving effective today, because, as Sir Richard Livingstone has pointed out, "In the past men accepted the Christian ideal even if they did not live the Christian life. A child born in the nineteenth century had its mind formed unconsciously by the atmosphere and beliefs around it. There is no such formative influence today, and to succeed in putting the Christian imprint upon the youth of this generation, we must find one." [3]

Christian forces have a moral as well as an educational crusade

[3] *On Education.* Used by permission of Cambridge University Press.

on their hands if in a field with such powerful competition they succeed in molding personality with "the stamp of Christ." Such an undertaking will require maximum effort and superior strategy.

MISTAKES IN STRATEGY

The strategy of the Christian forces seeking to develop Christian personality in youth must take into account its limitations, its opportunities, and its failures. Only a realistic view of the situation as it actually is will enable the work of Christian life making to expand in quantity and quality.

First it must recognize its limitations. The Christian strategy for education cannot resort to compulsion and control. Public education has this advantage, and education in the totalitarian countries has developed coercion to its ultimate and maximum capacity in effecting a way of life and a type of personality. But Christian education in the United States has neither the compulsion of law nor the momentum of universally accepted social tradition. It is not a must. Christian education is required to create its own opportunities. It exerts its influence only by an attractiveness which makes an individual appeal. Time is wasted in the circles of strategy by discussions of what ought to be people's attitudes and habits toward Christian education. We cannot scold people into religious instruction. Organized Christianity cannot disregard the conditions under which it must work and assume the attitude that it is just too bad for those who will not conform. How Christian education can develop its powers of attraction is the crux of the strategy needed to increase participation in its work.

Opportunity, however, presents an open door for contemporary Christian education in the United States. Freedom for religion not only to exist but to propagate makes effort the real determining factor in the results which Christian education achieves. The issue drawn between freedom to exist and freedom

25

to propagate in some totalitarian countries of Europe and some non-Christian countries of Asia may strike the United States eventually in the form of a religious tolerance which would make religious education a passive rather than an active factor in community life. However, at present no such restrictions exist here either by law or in the popular attitude. In fact, the climate of opinion is changing in ways which are favorable to increased religious activities. There is danger, however, that the new wine of an awakened need for spiritual development may be forced into the old bottles of yesterday's forms. A flexibility in adjusting to the current attitudes and responses of the present is a condition which makes this renewed religious interest an opportunity.

Much of the former and current strategy for developing character according to the Christian pattern will need serious appraisal. The record of its achievement in the light of its opportunity has not been brilliant. Important ground has been lost, and activities have appeared too often to be on dead center. A strategy which attracts only 60 per cent of the youth of grammar-school age, 40 per cent of the youth of high-school age, and 20 per cent of the youth of college age cannot be called an outstanding success.

The places of weakness and vulnerability in the Christian strategy must be brought to light and corrected.

There are at least four points in the current Christian strategy which indicate serious weakness and about which something can be done.

Certainly a survey of the resources devoted to the entire field of Christian education indicates that too little has been brought to the task. "Bricks cannot be made without straw." Yet the most important phase of education has had the least done for it. It is startling to realize how little Christian education has to work with. For every dollar spent on religion in the United States there are 750 spent for recreation. The situation at home is

similar to the description given to me by a newspaper corre-
spondent in Brazil with whom I was discussing the religious
needs and opportunities of that great country. He summed up the
Protestant activity by saying, "You are using a teaspoon when
you should be using a steam shovel."

Too often the Christian activity is the tragic story of getting
into the struggle too late. Christian education should come first
in a person's life and in the organization of the community. But
with increasing frequency this has not been the order. Parents
have said they will not force their children in religious matters,
although they do not hesitate to force them in health, social,
and intellectual matters. They of course do not make a distinction between guided activity and force. Then they look for a
scapegoat to blame for the 226-per-cent increase in juvenile
alcoholism in the last five years and for the 275,000 cases of
juvenile delinquency which get into our courts each year. These
parents are in the same category with Haggith, whose son
Adonijah made a mess of his life because "his father had never
at any time displeased him by asking, 'Why have you done thus
and so?'" (I Kings 1:6). And when life closed in on him, even
though then he ran and "caught hold of the horns of the altar,"
it was too late for religion to save him from the consequences of
bad education.

Organized religion has failed also because it did not "strike
while the iron [was] hot." Too much of our current preparation
is for yesterday's battles. Religion moves in last after the social
patterns of life are set, rather than first when it has the chance
to mold those patterns. In this respect church extension becomes
the beachhead for Christian education.

An appraisal of religious effort indicates that much of it is
fragmentary and sporadic. It is seasonal, specializing in religious-
emphasis weeks and go-to-church days. It is geared to emergen-
cies and crises rather than to the steady everyday drives which
determine the ultimate outcome. It marshalls its strength for the

sprint rather than the long pull. It recruits; then it does not train its recruits. It gathers its resources and then lets them spoil because of nonuse. Wars are won by the ability of forces to move on all battlefronts at once. But in matters of religion the strategy has tended to overemphasis in one phase with a corresponding underemphasis in some other phase. A study and application of Jesus' method in feeding the five thousand would go far to correct this weakness in current religious activity.

Then too a misunderstanding of the real meaning of tolerance has also contributed to the weakness of the Christian impact on life. Religion has given the impression that it is too easygoing. It does not impress its public with a sense of urgency. It lacks definiteness in defining its position. It hesitates to take positive and clear-cut stands. Often its attitude encourages people to make light of the sins which infect personal and social life and to undervalue the primacy of religion in all of life.

The strategy of evil has profited by this weakness in the Christian attitude. It was a major consideration in the Hitler strategy. Take a small advantage, Hitler said, which does not appear to be worth fighting for, until you have made so many small inroads that the opposition will not be able to defeat you when you make your major attack.

Every major moral and religious problem in personal or community living began as a little one which could have been easily dealt with if a firm and effective stand had been taken in the beginning.

MOLDING FORCES

If more lives are to be minted with the Christian imprint, all the areas where the work can be effectively performed must be alerted to the opportunities and reactivated for a maximum effort. Education has many channels through which its work is done. If it is to be Christian in its result, all these channels must be effectively utilized. Too often we think of Christian education as having only one channel of communication, namely, the church school. Society has attempted to clear itself of responsibility in Christian nurture by exalting, then neglecting, the church school as the sole instrument for its accomplishment.

There are, however, at least five channels through which such forces work upon personality. They are the home, the school, the community, the church, and the individual. Each offers an opportunity for influencing life which Christianity must utilize if it is to make a satisfactory imprint. Christianity, however, can make no claim for using any of them with maximum effectiveness at the present time.

The home has the first chance for making an imprint on the life of the child. According to Alfred North Whitehead for the first twelve years parents are the strongest influence upon children—for good or bad. In the matter of influence there are no neutral homes or parents. This is an ancient discovery about the influence of the home. The Hebrews knew and used it. A Hebrew child was taught the Ten Commandments before he could talk and was sent to the synagogue regularly for religious instruction at six. Augustine, who said that he drunk in as a baby the name of Christ with his mother's milk, credited this early Christian impression as a major factor in his reclamation as an adult.

The American home, however, has largely lost its consciousness as a molding center. While recognizing many very valuable functions for child development, the religious has been allowed to drop out. Its attributes have developed along secular rather than Christian lines.

The increasing consciousness toward the desirability of physical well-being and social acceptability among Americans has turned homemaking more in the direction of the stock-farm pattern than toward the Christian pattern. Much attention is paid to physical surroundings. Dwellings have become show places. The quality of housing has been greatly improved. Sanitary conditions, health procedures, body-building foods, school training, and social adjustment are now the studies of good parenthood. The pediatrician, the psychologist, and the psychiatrist are the special advisers of the homemakers. All of this, allowing for the proper discounting of the faddists and the commercializers, is to be commended. Nevertheless, a child with the best of this type of training and nothing more becomes an immature adult. He has strength without judgment or control or perception or motivation. The spiritual and the moral elements of his life have gone untended. The considerations in Jesus' early education, which concerned Joseph and Mary, are absent from much of modern home life. Parents today who ask Zechariah's and Elizabeth's question concerning the child John, "What then will this child be?" have an altogether different answer in mind. Their prayer, if they pray at all for their children, is for success and not for goodness.

The nuclei for Christian homemaking are widely distributed in our American communities. Multitudes of such homes now exist. They need, however, to become conscious of their community responsibility for molding sentiment in the Christian direction.

The public school gathers its importance as a molder of personality in two directions. It is professional. Its business is solely to educate, and its personnel is expertly trained. It is also monopolistic. It claims all the educable time of the child both in regular and in extracurricular activities. Here it has a priority supported by law. This favored position puts a heavy responsibility upon the school. It cannot escape a large measure of either praise or blame for the outcome.

Since it is so influential, what happens in it should not be left solely to the judgment of the professionals. All members of the community have the right to know what the school is doing and to evaluate its product. The Christian should be especially interested in its character development and spiritual nurture. Every parent and Christian worker should have some definite idea of what the schools in the community are doing along these lines.

In general, public education has developed five attitudes toward its moral and spiritual responsibilities. One is exclusive. It would exclude all religious aspects of education as not properly coming under its responsibility. This conception of public education has had strong professional support, and court decisions have indicated a definite trend toward legal support. However, the more apparent its results, the more frightening they have become, until an increasing group of educational experts are now warning the public against a pattern of national education which excludes religion.

Another theory of public education's responsibility to religion is compartmental. It puts religion in a form as a subject in the curriculum, or it makes religion a part of the elective extracurricular activities. Sometimes this gesture toward religion is more impressive than effective. You cannot judge a school's effectiveness in character building and spiritual nurture by the number of courses in religion which is offered. Education is a process of the whole personality. It cannot be accomplished through unrelated sections. The development of Christian personality has little chance in a system of education which may be one part religious and one hundred parts secular or pagan.

There is also the neutral idea toward religious development which is apparent in some school systems. It says to religion, "Leave us alone." It claims to be neither for nor against, so it ignores the whole matter of moral and spiritual development as a part of its educational processes. Such a position, while avoiding some difficult situations, usually creates greater ones for itself in the accumulated moral and character chaos which sooner or later catches up with it.

The influence of education as a character-building force was probably uppermost in the minds of our forefathers and accounts for the fact that specific directions for the inclusion of basic religious instruction in public education are absent from much of the early legislation. Our fathers assumed that the influence of instruction and instructors upon the student and the school community life would be Christian. Fortunately for many of us it has been. The number of teachers and administrators who recognize and cultivate the religious intangibles in public and higher education is a blessed community of educators to whom the quality of American living owes much. These are the men and women who create the atmosphere for Christian development. Better by far to have a faculty of high religious character teaching the secular subjects than to have a department of religion but no such supporting faculty in the other fields.

Currently the trend seems to be toward the co-operation theory of religious development as a part of public education, making it easier and more effective for the home and the church to give the supplemental religious instruction. Released time from the regular school day, co-operation in encouraging attendance, recognition of its value, and integrating it in the school life have produced excellent results in communities where parents and church groups contribute their full part to the plan.

The community also is a potent molder of character. Few realize the community's power to educate or what forces are at work in the community putting their stamp upon the people who live in it. A beautiful lawn can conceal a rattlesnake, and often our communities, having the outward appearances of desirability, have concealed in them the forces for character destruction.

Communities are good or bad forces in character education according to the institutions around which they are organized. Some institutions, commercial and social, create spiritual deficiencies, moral laxity, and ethical blindness. A reappraisal of a materially improved community life in which juvenile delinquency increases and crime costs rise to a new high of twenty billion dollars a year is urgently needed. The gambling racket has become a twelve-billion-dollars-a-year business with few respectable defenders. Nevertheless there seems to be little recognition of the fact that pinball, raffles, bingo, and the like, honey-combing our communities, are the bush leagues from which the major league of gambling is recruited.

The community itself is a positive influence either for good or for bad on character and personality development.

The church is a molder and an educator. Its sole business is to put upon personality the Christian imprint. Often it has been used as the whipping boy for the breakdown of character. Much such criticism is unwarranted. Often the church has failed because the community never gave it a chance. It has boxed the church in with inadequate resources and support. It has encouraged contrary influences. And it has withheld from it the best leadership and service.

Nevertheless the church must look to itself if it seeks to improve and increase its effectiveness. Adverse conditions cannot be used as an alibi. There are situations within the church which involve its own inherent vitality. Often it has not been insistent enough. It speaks with a weak voice for its position. It discounts its achievements and sells itself short. It has accepted a diet of crumbs and permitted criticism for its resultant weakness.

The church has not always been consistent in making good its claims. Its product has not always turned out as advertised. Before great issues it has at times stopped short of the position of its own logic. Between its preachments and its application to specific situations there is often an embarrassing discrepancy. Such looseness is character destroying. Parents need to recognize this in dealing with their children, and churches need to take it into account in dealing with the community.

The church is not always persistent in following through its positions. Its tendency is to blow hot and cold on moral, ethical, and spiritual issues. The perpetrators of evil know this and trade on it. The oratory of resolutions blows itself out before they reach their application to the problem itself. Performing the rites, the church too often fails to check up on the vows which go with the rites. Doing only the routine week after week, churches tend to become sterile rather than creative.

The church in its educational aspects needs bold revitalization.

Then the individual himself has something to say about the personality he will become. The Christian theory of growth makes a large place for self-determination and self-education. And while this position has been under strong current attack, the results in character are always attesting its truth. Human life is fashioned to go upstream. The process requires great personal effort, but it is possible and satisfying. A recognition of this personal power to effect changes in life for the better is essential if the terrible inferiority complex which the modern individual has concerning his own improvement is to be removed.

Certainly here is a conviction of our Puritan fathers which needs to be carried over into our age. They had a hopeful view of the outcome of life. William Lyon Phelps defined the difference in attitude between our age and the Puritan age by pointing out that each saw the same environment of filth and muck, but for us no good life can come out of it while for the Puritan it could produce the flower of Christian personality.

In these times of terrors, pains, miseries, regrets, vexations, and lassitudes, modern man can still find his deliverance in Wordsworth's discovery:

> The calm existence that is mine when
> I am worthy of myself.

THE FUTURE IS NOW

Perhaps the besetting sin of this generation is impatience. We want everything done in a hurry. But goodness is not a jiffy undertaking. It requires time to develop and spread. It is the work of decades and centuries. In the present we must, therefore, plan for the future. Today the shape of tomorrow's life takes form.

Therefore the task of this generation is crystal-clear. It is to set the pattern for the generations which follow. To make that life, the molds for the imprint of Christian character must be strengthened, improved, and multiplied. The neglected materials, our unchurched youth, must be recruited for the undertaking. Then with the urgency and resourcefulness of our Christian forebears this generation must get down to the business of making a better life and a better world realizable by the next generation, remembering at each stage of the task that the "life of a man . . . in God must bear the stamp of Christ" (Phillips).

1149397

CHAPTER II

THE MOLDERS

Manoah entreated the Lord, and said,
"O, Lord, I pray thee, let the man of God whom thou didst send
come again to us, and teach us what we are to do with the boy....
What is to be the boy's manner of life, and what is he to do?"
—JUDG. 13:8, 12

THE PRESENCE OF THE VERY YOUNG AND THEIR CURRENT STATUS in society present educational questions which cannot await leisurely answers. They demand attention at once because life is constantly changing and the disposition of these educational questions influence the nature of human growth. Where, however, these questions are taken to be answered is of paramount importance. The stamp on the future goes with the opportunity to answer them.

VITAL QUESTIONS IN EDUCATION

The ancient Manoah and his wife felt an urgency for the right answers to the educational questions which confronted them with the coming of their son. So they took the matter to God in prayer. Our day is inclined to make prayer the last rather than the first resort and God the forgotten authority in dealing with the important decisions of family life. Prayer itself has been neglected as one of the media of instruction. Conversation with God is more often thought of in child nurture as a source of deliverance rather than a means for guidance. We need to learn how to use prayer both for deliverance and for guidance in fulfilling our responsibility to the young. Manoah raised with God the vital questions for education in any age. His need for divine guidance in educational matters is indigenous to every culture and contemporary with every century.

Manoah asked five major questions which are basic to all education. First, what is the child to learn? The matter of selection begins with the birth of the child. Second, how is the child to be guided? The grooves of habit need help for the right start. Third, what is the child supposed to do? Action and reaction to life determine the later relations of social adjustment. Fourth, what is he to become? Destination cannot be left simply to chance. Fifth, who is to be his teacher? This is the question whose answer determines the answer to all the others.

When the right answers to these inquiries are in the possession of those who in various ways help to mold the life of the young, a good outcome can be confidently anticipated. These are the definitive questions which must be asked of all modern educational activities, and the nature of the answer is the standard by which the validity of these educational activities in home, church, community, and school must be judged. They touch the spots in the developing life of youth which put the final stamp upon personality. Their consideration calls for an examination of the entire field of modern education.

ASPECTS OF EDUCATION

To arrive at the right answers, the molders of character—parents, teachers, citizens—must have a clear conception of what education really is. On the popular and superficial side education is thought of in terms of helpful habits, efficient skills, adequate training, and social polish. These are the current demands by which our educational systems are being judged. Social acceptability, economic competence, and manual dexterity are the total results many look for in the education of themselves or of their children. But these are the superficial and the lower aspects of human development. Good manners, the ability to make money, and a cleverness in muscular and mental co-ordination, which gives grace and skill to bodily movements, do not touch the heart and character and personality of the person thus trained. Such development is possible on the animal level of life. A dog can be taught to become socially acceptable, to get his own living, and to be quick and clever in all his movements; yet, as Chesterton pointed out, whoever would think of asking even an exceptionally trained dog what he was going to be when he grew up? Yet how often are these results all we look for and demand in the education we get for ourselves or the education we provide for our children. These qualities of life are the attributes of training, and they are very valuable. However, education goes deeper into life than the external aspects of training. Education to be effective must develop insights, encourage reflection, insure right choices, and arrive at sound judgments. Education must concern itself not only with what we do but with what we become, and religious education must go beyond the inculcation of the forms of godliness to the quickening of the spirit of godliness.

It is necessary to keep in mind this distinction between education as training and education as development if we are to make the Christian imprint a part of the fabric of personality rather than a superficial habit pattern of life. The markings of true Christian education can never be completely eradicated from life even though under certain adverse circumstances they may be blurred and hidden. On the other hand, however, when we see the practices of Christianity quickly and easily sloughed off by persons who for much of their lifetime have been participants in the church's activities and program, we must conclude that their form of godliness had come more from the training of social pressure than from the education of the spirit.

The two most-quoted leaders in the field of twentieth-century general education confirmed this deeper view of true education and warned against the insidious deceptions of the superficial view. John Dewey held that the educated person must possess the "ability to discriminate, to make decisions which penetrate beneath the surface, to know the difference between froth and reality, between sound and sense, between the conspicuous and the important, the emphatic and the distinctive." Whitehead supported this position with his description of an educated person, whom he held must possess the ability to analyze, to assemble, to generalize, and to evaluate the facts related to his life.

IMPLICATIONS FOR CHRISTIAN EDUCATION

This distinction between training and development in education, when applied to the Christian growth of life, carries with it serious challenge and new hope. Much of what has passed for Christian education we must recognize as only a type of social training and conventional reaction which rubs off under the pressure of changing group activity. It has been satisfied to accept approved conduct in place of spiritual growth. In all sincerity it has sought to leave its Christian imprint on life, but the impression has not held. The ills of present-day society bear witness to this type of educational inadequacy.

Why we are failing to put a sustained Christian imprint upon life and what is required to make our Christian education more effective will appear with an appraisal of past procedures and a recognition of present trends.

Frequently on the local and individual level Christian education has not had a definite pattern. It has been left largely to take its course. The five fundamental questions which Manoah raised have not been considered by parents planning for the education of their children nor communities in providing for the total education of their young. Christian education on these levels

39

has been with few exceptions a haphazard procedure with success resulting more often from chance than from preparation.

The blame for past failures should not be laid solely on the doorstep of the home and the church. In their reactions they have been influenced by popular facts and theories in education too strong at the time to be overcome. Religious education has had to battle its way against a philosophy of general education which has overemphasized self-expression and underemphasized guidance and discipline. It has been surrounded by an educational atmosphere which has given the children what they want under the guise of making education enjoyable. It has been confronted with the popular standard of mediocrity, which, of course, is incompatible with Christlikeness. It has competed with a system whose requirements were minimums, with rewards and approval based on school and community popularity contests rather than on character and intellectual achievements. Christian education, fighting often for its very life in an educational setup which granted it little place, has had to make concessions to this prevailing philosophy or be more completely ostracized and ensmalled.

The results have forced a reconsideration of the validity and effectiveness of this pseudo-democratic theory of self-expression in education. And what has been uncovered is not at all reassuring. It hasn't made for social stability nor for individual maturity. Emotional immaturity and the emphasis on unrestrained indulgence have increased the divorce rate to one for every three marriages and multiplied the number of broken homes. Psychic instability now claims one out of five. The adolescent intellect has made ours a totalitarian age. Social maladjustment has increased adult tensions and nurtured juvenile delinquency. Why should these be the outcomes when we are giving both youth and adults more education than any previous generation has received? And the facts are forcing the conviction that our philosophy of education has been at fault. These modern tragedies in living stem back to the cause of Adonijah's downfall. He came to grief because "his father had never at any time displeased him by asking, 'Why have you done thus and so?'" (I Kings 1:6).

Edward Carpenter in his biography of Paul shows what has happened to the youth of today who are the products of this current educational philosophy. "Free to become themselves," he says, "each goes his own way and there is no home to which he returns. The operative word is 'expression.' The parent waters and never disciplines the tender plant but allows it to shoot out its leaves wherever it will, although they may obscure other people's sight of the sun and what nasty children they usually become." [1]

We are driven to the frightful conclusion that we have been doing something to life through education which is actually self-destroying and that only a long period of re-education can correct it. Omar Bradley touched the spot of our vulnerability when in a Boston speech he said, "Ours is a world of secular giants and ethical infants."

The task before Christian education in correcting our arrested spiritual development is further complicated by a warped perspective of what the people of this age most need. Our age is not conscious of the nature of its failing. Like the people to whom Confucius spoke, our age has been "trained to be dissatisfied with a deformed finger, but not to recognize that it should be dissatisfied about its deformed mind." This may account for the fact that we spend more money to eliminate pain than we do to eliminate sin.

The facts are plain and conclusive. The product does not come up to the Christian standard. The trouble is also apparent. The process and not the material is to blame.

There is danger that a frightened and horrified public opinion

[1] *That Man Paul* (Longmans, Green & Co.). Used by permission of the publisher.

41

will aggravate rather than rectify the condition by resorting to emotional outbursts of criticism. To be sure, the conduct and the viewpoints of increasing numbers of our youth cannot be condoned and should be openly condemned. It is also an obligation of the Christian position to include the individual in fixing responsibility. We cannot relieve youth of its responsibility for its derelictions on the argument that they are the victims of their times. Christianity holds that all ages must live above and against their times in maintaining Christian standards. Youth is no exception, nor does it want to be. The appeal to discipline for a sufficient motive finds a response in youth.

However, we must not ignore the factors which are fundamentally at fault in producing our present sub-Christian standard of living. To do nothing about those factors thwarts any other effort which may intend to correct the condition. Good material may be spoiled by poor workmanship. It can never offset improper casting. So the first conditions to consider in stamping the Christian pattern on life are the molders and the molds, the skill and fidelity of the molder and the precision and correctness of the mold.

What of our teachers—that vast group in all walks of life who by precept and example, as well as by the decisions which determine personal and social conduct, direct our young in the ways they should go? And what about the molds, those patterns of conduct, those ways of living, which put upon human action the stamp of refinement or crudity, decency or vulgarity, sincerity or pretense, morality or immorality, quality or mediocrity, God or Mammon, Christ or Caesar? Wrong patterns recast the German youth completely in the short period of a decade. What happens to a child in his first seven years stamps indelible imprints that are never eradicated according to the educational authorities of a great section of the world's religious life.

Correction and restraint are emergency measures in dealing with the defective expressions of Christian living. They are very necessary and are often unintelligent and neglected. But the avoidance of defects in the products goes back to the molder and his molds.

The teacher is the key. Into his hands the materials are first committed. He is the trustee for their protection and preservation. He works them into their first patterns of living. He also creates the conditions for their place and usefulness in life. Here again we need to be reminded that the term "teacher" in this connection cannot be given a narrowly professional definition. The molders of youth are all whose contact leaves an impression on youth.

It is a strong and uncomfortable doctrine which puts the chief responsibility for the maladjustments and delinquencies of youth as citizens upon the teachers. But it is an old one. The Chinese experience created the proverb "If youth goes wrong, arrest the teacher"; and from one of the earliest discoveries of the Hebrews in the field of education came the observation that "as their fathers did, so they do" (II Kings 17:41).

If, therefore, we are going to improve the quality of both living and its expression in society, we must look first to those who teach. What manner of person shall the parent teacher, the professional teacher, the citizen teacher, be?

THE CHRISTIAN TEACHER

Whatever our Christian teaching function and opportunity may be in relation to youth, we must "remember that we who are [Christian] teachers will be judged by a much higher standard" (Jas. 3:1 Phillips) than those whose teaching responsibilities are determined by secular considerations. Those who would impress on others the Christian imprint must themselves bear the Christian imprint. While this requirement may appear too obvious even to mention, the fact remains that often the cause of a faulty character product is not due so much to faulty methods as to faulty persons. And frequently character is put in a secondary category when the qualifications of good teachers are considered. In filling the teaching posts in our church schools we are so hard pressed to find sufficient candidates that character and ability must often yield their place of first consideration to availability and willingness. Parents likewise defeat their highest purpose for their children when they fail to recognize that the one thing they can do for them is the best thing they can do for them, namely, live in their presence the life they would have their children emulate. And professional teaching still struggles with the question of religion in education because its approach is from the direction of methods and laws rather than by way of the persons who teach. Departments of religion and Bible courses offered for academic credit do not insure a Christian school atmosphere or an educated Christian. The distinction between religious education and religious instruction must be kept in mind. Nor is the delicate balance between the function of church and state the area where the struggle will be won to make our education produce the good life. One man of God teaching chemistry can do more for the religious life of a school than a whole department of religion offering simply academic and professional courses in religion.

Manoah had it right. We must find the man of God and put him in charge if we expect the highest possible result in character and personality.

Furthermore, both precedent and experience validate a return to this position.

Colonial America saw clearly where and what the teacher should be in developing their "holy experiment" of creating a new "nation, under God." The teacher in the church was placed beside the preacher, with equal consideration given to the employment of both. And doctrine was equally evaluated with ability in the selection of those who were to teach, indicating that in the judgment of the Fathers a proper philosophy of life was the basic requirement in teaching and that ability and training were to implement the teacher's philosophy of life but not to substitute for it. Such an attitude estopped a consideration of the separation of church and state as a legal question. But as James H. Nichols pointed out, it did not "weaken the hold of Christian ideology and morals on [the] community." [2] How far we have departed from this standard for the qualification of all teaching is quite evident in the inferior type of life our total teaching effort is producing.

The Roman Catholic Church has held persistently despite popular trends in education to the position that what a person is determines what a person teaches. The manner in which this church expresses this position is debatable. We are not dealing with that in this connection. What, however, they have done about it should be warning to Protestants in the face of our neglect. The Roman Catholic religious order of teachers outnumbers their priests by two to one. On that basis we should have 400,000 full-time religious teachers in the Protestant churches and according to the best estimates we now have about 10,000.

The conclusion seems clear to educators such as Clyde Lemont Hay, who finds the blind spot in Protestant education to be our indifference to its predominant secular approach. He is convinced that "Protestantism cannot long maintain its position in American culture while it continues to allow its children to grow up in religious illiteracy." And he rightly concludes that the "focal point in the education of a Christian is well-guided teachers." [3]

We add to this one other danger, namely, that teachers and teaching will be thought of in too narrow terms so that they

[2] "Separation of Church and State," *The Christian Century*, Mar. 3, 1948.
[3] *The Blind Spot in American Public Education* (The Macmillan Co.).

do not include the home and the community, as well as the school and the church, and that they relieve parents and citizens from their responsibility to be teachers by a purely professional attitude toward the teaching function.

THE CHRISTIAN TEACHER'S GUILD

Christian teachers should become conscious of their identity and of their diversity.

Many who because of their position cannot escape the teaching function do not think of themselves as teachers of others. They would disavow the designation if confronted with it. In all sincerity they think of teaching and teachers in terms of specialization. They think, because they have no classroom assigned, no teacher's certification, no subject to teach, that they have no pupils and no interest in or responsibility for teaching. Parents are tempted to think of themselves more often as providers than as teachers. Executives in an absorption for business success overlook the importance of the impression they make upon their employees. Preachers succumbing to the subtle attitudes of professionalism can hamper their effectiveness by putting a greater emphasis upon their words than their deeds. Thus they often dissipate the power of a great sermon on Sunday by an indifferent observance of its precepts in their own lives on Monday. To use technical language, they are didactic and not empirical. They say, but they do not show. The citizen outside his special relation to family, church, or employment is doing far more teaching than he supposes. He is a watched person, leaving impressions upon the lives of many to whom he is nameless. A trip to a department store, a journey on a train, a walk upon a busy street, are unconsciously for the participant a day of teaching. In fact it is good teaching only when, like the little Pippa, it is unconscious influence through the spontaneous expression of natural goodness.

We have a penchant in the United States for the observance of special days. Many of them are trivial in their occasion and commercial in their purpose. But I can see how "I Am a Teacher Day" could be transformingly revolutionary in its long-range results if properly presented and promoted.

The identification of all Christians with their teaching function is a first step in placing the Christian imprint upon life.

Such identification not only brings to light the diversity of the approach which can be made in achieving the Christian character and personality objective, but also uncovers resources for the work which have been overlooked and therefore unemployed. A narrow professional point of view regarding teaching leaves the Church in a very pessimistic mood. Good religious teachers are few, and the need is great. Like the disciples such a consideration argues the wisdom of giving up. What are our few professionals among so many uneducated Christians and non-Christians? But a realization that in varying degrees of ability and opportunity all are teachers greatly increases the Protestant teachers' stock pile.

The specialists are one group, very small in number, but very important in the service they render. Now there is one for every 6,000 Protestants. We have not developed them in any like number to the Roman Catholics and the Jews. By Roman Catholic standards we are now at least 400,000 short in full-time teaching specialists. So those we have must become directors and administrators rather than teachers.

These professionals do not, however, encompass or represent the total Protestant teaching strength. To make a comprehensive survey of the Christian teaching that is being done, we must see the relation of all occupational groups to the task of placing the Christian imprint upon life. Likewise to judge its effectiveness, we must grade their works.

The public-school teacher cannot avoid being a religious influence. His influence may be positive or negative. It may be good or bad. But one thing is certain—it cannot be neutral. Neutrality in religion is a fallacy on which much of the argument for no religion in our school and college systems is based. The school as an institution of the state must be neutral in religious matters, we are told. But the Master's dictum still has its application to our educational philosophies and their implementations—"He who is not with me is against me." So the teacher in so-called secular education becomes a force either for or against the objectives of religious education regardless of law. The intangibles of character, attitude, and conduct determine on which side the teacher's influence shall register. There is therefore a tremendous volume of sound Christian education taking place in public schools and college halls which does not bear the trademark, but which is nonetheless genuine. Perhaps it cannot be measured and will never show up in a statistical statement, but it is a considerable asset which can be counted on and should be recognized and appreciated.

Consideration should be given to who teaches as well as what is taught if Christian character and personality are the products we seek through education. And often the cart is put before the horse in determining the qualifications which would make a teacher most likely to succeed.

The ministry supplies another large segment in the guild of Christian teachers. While the modern Protestant pastor is likely to think more of the preaching and administrative function than the teaching function of his work, his divine commission calls for both. In this the "servant is not greater than his master" (John 13:16), and the Master's commission was both to teach and to preach. Actually a good case can be made out for the primacy of the teaching function of the ministry. It is the necessary foundation for all that a minister seeks to do through preaching and administration. Teaching affects the heart and the will as well as the mind. It enlightens the understanding; it improves the skills; it opens avenues of thought and action. These are the means for a full and complete Protestant ministry.

Here again a narrow interpretation of method deflects the minister from the realization of the ways through which he can teach. Popular thought associates a teaching pastor with a Sunday-school class or a church-training group. Sometimes a pastor is thought to be indifferent to religious education in the church because he does neither of these. They are opportunities which if properly selected can do great good under skilled ministerial leadership. However, they by no means constitute the largest contribution a preacher can make through a teaching ministry. The improvement of his people will depend upon his resourcefulness in using every contact as a means for teaching without permitting the effort to appear evident. People react unfavorably when the didactic finger is pointed at them. But in the quiet and unobtrusive ways of the Master Teacher a modern pastor through his coming as counselor, friend, and leader can guide his people into all truth; and that is the finest fruitage of a teaching ministry.

A mother once said to me that she would rather have her children attend the church service than the Sunday school, and the reason she gave was the demoralizing character of the conduct of that particular Sunday school in contrast to the effectiveness of the church service as a medium of religious education. Public worship, prayer, scripture reading, music, and preaching are all powerful educational instruments in the hands and under the direction of a skillful minister who is conscious of their educational objective and value.

The divine commission directs the preacher *to go* and *to teach*.

Life commitment to Christian service automatically makes a person a teacher in the school of Christian life. Once committed the objective of a career is lifted from a material to a spiritual

49

level, from the accumulation of things to the development of the good life. Things become the means for a higher accomplishment. It was said of a prominent manufacturer at the turn of the century that in his factory he made money and shoes and men. To the purely commercial aspects of his career he added the real commitment of his life, which was to provide the means, the knowledge, the desire, and the example that those for whom he had some responsibility might share also in the spiritual profits of abundant living. The profit-sharing schemes of the twentieth century have for the most part confined themselves to physical and material welfare and ignored or denied any responsibility for a plan of employment which results in spiritual profit sharing and the improvement of life itself. As business and professional people too many of us have made "money and shoes" and have neglected the opportunity and obligation to invest our lives also in making men. This, it seems to me, is the distinctive aspect of the commitment of life to Christian service. The investment of life in a place or a profession is incidental to an understanding of this higher assignment. They simply provide a medium through which we work toward this higher goal. A committed doctor becomes more than a healer of bodily ills. Through his position and opportunity he becomes a physician to the human spirit as well. It was a very wise dean of a medical school who advised premedical students to take courses in Bible and religion and philosophy. They provide a preparation without which a physician's healing skill may never reach its maximum power.

So it is with all other occupations of life. Call it the overtones of one's activities or whatever you will, it is in fact a teaching service from which we cannot escape and through which a life committed to Christian service finds meaning in its commitment and opportunity to fulfill it.

The Christian teaching guild includes also a large host of

amateur volunteers of whom it can be said that they are a "great multitude which no man could number, from every nation, from all tribes and peoples and tongues" (Rev. 7:9). No real estimate of Protestant teaching strength can be arrived at without giving full credit to the work of this group. They actually carry Protestantism's heaviest teaching load. To them we must turn for more and better service in producing the Christian imprint. In our Protestant church schools alone there are more than three million volunteers working as teachers and officers. In the related Protestant-sponsored activities of the church and community devoted to character training, there are another three million engaged in impressing the Christian imprint upon the personalities of the forty million youth who are the special Protestant responsibility. One such teacher for every thirteen young people in the nation is an encouraging ratio provided their opportunities to serve in this capacity are increased and their training improved for performing this task. The basic resources for achieving the Christian purpose in character are already at work.

The family is a teaching factor in molding character and developing personality which needs in the United States to be brought more consciously into the circle of the Christian teaching guild. Older cultures utilize the family for educational purposes in ways which the American family ignores and resents. Historically and universally the family has had much to do with what might be called the education for life. It has substituted for the school when necessity required, and it has supplemented formal education in fixing character traits. The Hebrew family was and still is an educational unit. The oriental home continues to be a place of learning where the grandmother is likely to exercise the largest influence. Ruth McKenney called Paris a city of civilized children and credited it to the fact that the child's education in France is a co-operative project with the whole family competing for the privilege to participate. There amid the atmosphere of "loving kindness; plus the most constant and anxious attention" the most important part of these children's lives takes place. And where we Americans assume that the grown-up atmosphere of the family is boring and retarding to the child, France, Mrs. McKenney observes, demonstrates that it produces happier children with fewer problems of social adjustment than our increasing insistence that children's education in all its phases must be a self-initiated activity conducted in the "society of their peers." [4]

The inescapable role of teacher is the lot of every parent. "As parents we are engaged in teaching our children whether we want to or not. Beat them, coddle them, ignore them, worry about them, love them, or hate them, you are still teaching them," says Gilbert Highet. In his book *The Art of Teaching* he reminds parents that their relationship to their children is "essentially based on teaching" and that "in a society full of vague and confused people too many of us fail to teach our own children something sure and reliable."

All of this brings a reassuring significance to the work of Christian education. Not only does it support the contention that it must have a larger place in developing life, but it challenges groups often unmindful of their teaching function to direct this function to good purposes. It also contributes greatly to the confidence of success in the effort to make the good life a normal and abiding imprint.

To the participants in the teacher's guild for the Christian imprint, there should also come a sense of fellowship and cooperation in their educational task. "The eye cannot say to the hand, 'I have no need of you'" (I Cor. 12:21.) Nor can one group say to another, "This is your business. What is that to us? See thou to it." Nor can the common objective be reached through criticism of one group by the other. An examination

[4] "Paris! City of Children," *Holiday*, Apr., 1953.

would clearly indicate that in respect to our effectiveness we "all have sinned and fall short of the glory of God" (Rom. 3:23) in the task of moral and spiritual development. The home blaming the school and the school blaming the church and the church blaming both destroy unity of effort and the co-ordination necessary for the maximum result. Each branch in the guild of Christian teachers needs the understanding, support, and encouragement of the other branches.

THE CHRISTIAN TEACHER'S PREPARATION

Professionalism in one field does not carry with it expertness in all others, nor do a right spirit and a sincere desire substitute for a lack of technical and professional preparation. From both these popular fallacies the work of Christian character development has suffered. For secular education we say only the best in training and preparation, but for Christian education how often does it appear that anything goes. We need to face the facts involved in the realization that a college degree and sometimes a theological degree do not qualify a person for the Christian teaching responsibilities in the home, church, school, and community. It is just as basic to good teaching to assume that a doctor of philosophy degree in chemistry does not in itself prepare a person to teach religion as it is to insist that a degree in chemistry does not qualify a person to teach history. And while attitude and spirit are far more important factors in successful teaching than our current quantitative standards allow, yet "zeal without knowledge" is a bungling destroyer against which the early Church's most highly educated and effective organizer warned.

If the Christian imprint is our intention, then we should consider carefully the qualifications required of those who would successfully impress that imprint through their contacts. In fact the standards which qualify a person to take over the work of Christian teaching are more demanding then the standards required for other types of teaching. Paul reminds us that "we who are [Christian] teachers will be judged by a much higher standard." The Christian teacher has the double necessity of meeting both religious and secular requirements. He must have both spirit and skill. He must live a life as well as teach its philosophy. He must know God as well as books and people. This dual requirement was an early discovery of those who sought to leave God's imprint upon the life of their day. To Moses we are indebted for the earliest and still adequate standards for successful service in this field. Looking for effective workers in establishing the society of the people of God, the Lord certified Bezalel to Moses by saying, "I have filled him with the Spirit of God, with ability and intelligence, with knowledge and all craftsmanship" (Exod. 31:3). And this yardstick for measuring the qualifications of those who must work on the supreme religious task needs no modernization. It stands in the category of a truth once delivered. It says all that needs to be said on the subject of qualifications. And when you find such a person, you can trust him with the great responsibility of society's future.

The qualifications most needed in the workers with character and personality in home, church, school, and community are still the four which Bezalel possessed. The measure of success is the ability, intelligence, skill, and spirit of the workmen. Their presence must be looked for and cultivated. Where they are dormant, they must be quickened. Where they are limited, they must be supplemented. Where they are at work, they must be encouraged. If parents would see and seek these qualities in the fulfillment of their parenthood, the school and the church would have a better chance; and their children would develop under such preparation an immunity to moral and spiritual diseases of community life.

The achievements of many of our church schools would move out of the red of failure or mediocrity if these requirements were made the basis of teacher selection. Has he some ability? Is he endowed with an intelligence which is recognized through alertness, resourcefulness, and common sense? Has he skill in craftsmanship, and will he take training either to acquire or to improve it? Has he the spirit of God, which is something vastly different from a knowledge of God or the forms of a personal brand of godliness?

It may be too much to expect this age to subordinate its mechanical and material goals in life to the investments which should be made in human personalities. But if citizenship responsibility could be associated in the popular thinking with teaching opportunity, the primary characteristics of good community life would begin to appear and the corollary benefits would inevitably follow. We must learn that the fruitage of life is not a synthetic production. It grows out of a life which has sprung from carefully selected seeds and cultivated by faithful and loving hands.

Would you then make everybody schoolmasters? My answer is that everybody now for good or ill is a schoolmaster. I would make them schoolmasters after the pattern of Christ.

THE TEACHER'S TEACHER

It is of course evident that when we lift up these qualifications of ability, intelligence, skill, and spirit as the attributes of the Christian teacher and personalize them in the lives of parents and teachers in particular and citizens in general, we have created a major teaching responsibility for everybody.

Such a teacher must have a teacher, since such a leader must always be a follower. To whom we turn for a pattern of expression is as important as the dedication of our talents to the task.

John Colet, a schoolmaster of fifteenth-century England, whose name still shines in the galaxy of the world's great teachers, had placed over his desk chair a portrait of Christ inscribed with the words "Learn of me." The portrait, hung where the teacher did his preparation and where the students came for instruction, served a double purpose. It reminded the man of his master Teacher and the boys of their master Model. Thus while prepared to teach others, John Colet was not forgetting Paul's admonition to teach himself something.

Artists, I am told, learn the rudiments of painting and then study with a master that they might catch his spirit. They seek to discover what it is in the master himself which transmits quality and immortality to his canvases. So it has been with all who have devoted successfully their talents of ability, intelligence, skill, and spirit to the artistry of life. In the presence of the master they have come upon the secret which produces the Christian imprint from within and sets it so that the wear and tear of living cannot tarnish or remove it.

For the Christian teacher in all the stations of life Jesus is that master. In his person he demonstrated the highest development of humanity, and in his relations with others he practiced the methods by which his life and teaching reached them and made them over into his image.

Those who seek to leave the Christian imprint on others must not overlook the One who fulfills the double role of perfect model and perfect teacher. He alone is the perfect divine pattern. We cannot go beyond him. In this artistry of life he is the master whose touch all others can hope only to approximate.

While in methods of human approach he has much to teach us, his own uniqueness as an artist, putting himself into the human canvases on which he worked, was an inwardness of spirit which has to be felt rather than charted and caught rather than taught. In the character of Christ we find the secret of his expertness. Only as we live in his presence with eager expectation and real humility can we hope to gather some of it to ourselves. Sometimes we can be lead to sense it through some life which has itself been remade into a closer conformity to this divine pattern, just as Peter found him through the medium of his brother Andrew. Often we must see him through a flash experience such as opened Paul's eyes and made him a master workman. But always we must keep some time in the busy workdays of our Christian living to learn of him.

CHAPTER III

THE MOLDING PURPOSE

*You have taken away the key of knowledge;
you did not enter yourselves, and you
hindered those who were entering.*
—LUKE 11:52

THERE ARE SIGNS IN THE ACTIVITIES AND ATTITUDES OF THE present which indicate that Christian education will have a new day of opportunity. It is therefore very important that those who educate, those who provide for education, and those who are educated should have clearly in mind the valid purpose of education.

During the decades of 1920 to 1950 Christian education as a part of the total educational enterprise was in greater or less eclipse. It was overshadowed in importance by education for social and utilitarian purposes. It was ruled off many college campuses by a pseudo intellectualism. It was ridiculed by a society for whom war had destroyed moral inhibitions and the taste for good things. It was feared and attacked by political leaders who knew that they could never come to power so long as the guiding hand of Christianity was felt in education. Likewise it "was wounded in the house of [its] friends" (Zec. 13:6); for unchristian philosophies of education, then popular, invaded the philosophy and methods of Christian education at many points and in many subtle ways, which sapped its power and altered its spirit.

All in all, Christian education had a hard time during much of the first half of the twentieth century. To say the least, it was treated as the stepchild of education and repressed until it developed a serious inferiority complex. Instead of asserting its rights, it spent its strength defending itself. It lost its sense of confidence, which was replaced by an inner feeling of uncertainty. It no longer spoke with assurance. Even the existence of God came to be a matter of scientific opinion and marketplace debate.

It was also ridiculed by the other members of the educational family for its "hand me-down" methods, its "cast-off" equipment, its amateur pedagogy, its quaint and old-fashioned ideas about life, and its "unliberated" view of morals. No wonder Christian education got an inferior view of itself and expressed it. The very fact that it kept belittling itself in public encouraged the public to take Christian education at its own estimate.

Christian education was literally starved during this period. It got only the crumbs under the table of a sumptuous educational board. These crumbs consisted of poor equipment, insufficient and unusable time, and inferior teaching. It got the leftovers from the wild and prodigal life of a sensual and materialistic era.

The result was to be expected. Christian education declined and society suffered. At first people were not conscious of what was happening to them. The deteriorating effects were both gradual and subtle. Furthermore, the capacity for self-analysis is never great and is likely to be exercised only when life reaches a desperation *in extremis*.

Christian education lost numbers and quality during those three decades. At points in doctrine and method it compromised with the world. It fell into the trap which secular educationalists had set unwittingly for themselves, of identifying a method of procedure with a philosophy of life. Thus many educational rediscoveries such as behaviorism, which might have had some value as a method, became instruments of death because they were accepted as a clue to origin and meaning.

The one great source of strength which Christian education has, namely, its distinctiveness, was softened as a concession to twentieth-century progress, with the hope that becoming like all other education it might be accepted on equal terms in the educational family. This of course, proved to be untrue. The greater the compromise, the less respect came to Christian education. Therefore it declined while all other education advanced.

Now in retrospect we see the seeds of many of the evils which beset this day watered, if not planted, by the attitudes of Christian education during and following the First World War. The wartime code of morality, which sanctioned practices and attitudes offering only immediate benefits, found no sharp challenge in the moral and ethical discipline inculcated by the Church. There also could be found the influences of a relativism which sanctioned accommodations in conduct to fit the mood of the times. Its important emphasis upon the social gospel did in its application deflect attention from an individual responsibility which demanded a personal choice and required personal standards. The quality of life was, therefore, neglected by an absorbing concern for the conditions of living. Comfort, which had been denied to so many, instead of righteousness became the goal of life. Self-indulgence overwhelmed the efforts of self-denial. Morality was redefined as the device of social adjustment rather than the character of God revealed in the life of Christ.

The price of human control, therefore, sunk to the sensate level. It could be bought in exchange for the creature comforts. Political enslavement, social evil, and character deterioration found human defenses down and counterforces confused and demoralized. Man lost his sense of dignity and his self-respect. And when he came to the awful realization of where and what he was, there was no voice either within his heart or in the life around him which could shame him as it did the prodigal with the stabbing truth that he was meant to be something better because he was his Father's son.

Christian education became, to be sure, a victim during these wayward years in human history; but much of the discrediting reaction to it grew out of its own attitudes and strategy.

HOPE IN THE PRESENT

We must not, however, permit a discouraging analysis of the past to deflect us from seeing and appraising the hopeful evidence for the future. Current changes in attitude and conditions indicate that Christian education will have an opportunity in the future. The changing state of the public mind is on its side. The acceptance of the principle of education for all as a human right and a social necessity gives Christian education a basis for popular appeal which it did not formerly have. If Paul were here now, he would make the most of this favorable mind-set regarding education as he did in Athens when, sensing the popular interest in the pagan gods, he used the opportunity to reveal the true God.

The generosity of the public purse for education has already reacted to the advantage of Christian education. While 1953 showed the largest expenditure for public education in the history of the United States (more than seven billion dollars), it also set a like record in expenditures for improving and enlarging the equipment for religious education.

The discovery that more than half of the world's population is illiterate and the realization of the awful consequences have unquestionably directed attention to the world's religious illiteracy and its devastating consequences. To know what the situation actually is forms the first step in dealing with it.

The development of the Laubach method for teaching the three *R*'s in a mass attack on the scourge of illiteracy will give religious education rapidly increasing opportunities in the mission fields. It will also necessitate a definite change in the religious approach. Already more than sixty million people have rapidly been taught to read by this method, and it is now working in 250 languages. Within the next quarter of a century illiteracy can be eliminated among the young and significantly reduced among older groups.

In those countries which will be affected this change from illiteracy to literacy will increase both opportunity and competition for religious education. The printed page will become a widely usable instrument in religious instruction. But antagonistic ways of life such as Communism and the indigenous religious and political philosophies will also use the printed page. They will compete for the minds liberated from the dungeons of illiteracy. Already they are doing this with telling effect among the groups who can read. They are flooding the distribution centers with a variety of literature sold within the price range of these impoverished people or given free to them and written in words which can be understood amid the conditions in which these people live. Neither Christianity nor democracy has met this challenge as yet effectively. Their literature is too expensive, too limited in scope, too Western in point of view, and too unrealistic in the application of their principles to the immediate situation which confronts the population. Religious education should be experimenting in this field now, and the background support necessary to utilize this opportunity in the largest possible way should be cultivated. Here the Christian Church has had fair warning. Another tragedy because of the too-little too-late policy can be avoided if the proper steps are now taken to be ready and adequate as a literate generation replaces its illiterate fathers.

The chapter in education now being written by the activities of the Christian Church around the world is a cause for hope. While many nations have adopted the principle of education for all, even the older and more established nations have never assumed full responsibility for its provision. Parochial and private schools take over a large part of this task even in the education-ally favored nations such as the United States and Great Britain. In fact in the United States 30 per cent of all education of college grade or higher is either church sponsored or church supported.

In the democracies such as India, Nationalist China, and Korea, where illiteracy runs as high as 80 per cent, the problems of cost and trained leadership make the principle of education for all impossible of immediate accomplishment through government provision alone. Here the serious efforts of the governments are being largely supplemented by church-sponsored schools on all educational levels, and more help of this nature is being wel-comed by the governments of these nations. This problem of illiteracy bears closely upon the life of the United States. Even nearby Puerto Rico, so vitally identified with the United States, has the problem of providing education for all. Although it is guaranteed by the constitution and administered by a sincere government up to the limit of its financial ability, there are still more than 300,000 children of school age to say nothing of illiterate adults in a population of 2,500,000 for whom educa-tional provision has not been made. At present and for some time to come supplemental help must be supplied by the church schools if education in Puerto Rico is provided for all.

The danger, however, in any dual system of education lies in the threat of dominance by one of the parties participating. When church and state take part in public education, a totali-tarian position by either one defeats the uses of education for the development of political democracy and individual freedom. The Church's activity in education is being examined by the younger democracies from this angle.

If these governments appear to be oversensitive in limiting the frame within which the educational activities of the Church may operate, their position should be judged in the light of past history. The Church in its two main branches has conducted its general educational activities from two quite different motivations. The Roman Catholic branch has sought control as basic to the success of its educational program. The Protestant branch has made improvement its motivation for the schools it establishes in the countries needing supplemental assistance for their educational needs. These points of view represent a fundamental difference in fixing the authority for knowledge. They are being scrutinized by the countries now faced with a scarcity of school facilities before accepting the educational help of the Church. It is also an underlying consideration in the current discussion of the place of religion in public education in the United States. The concern of the Church should be for conditions which would give Christian education a fair chance to develop the spirit and to commend its truth to those who must make a decision regarding a way of life.

On the basis of this eagerness for intellectual development the Church has a real opportunity now in the countries awakening to the need of education for all. Entering the educational field for this purpose can be justified as necessary if the ability for intelligent decisions in all matters pertaining to life, including religion, is the objective. On the other hand, the religious attitude which seeks full control of education either directly or indirectly for doctrinal, political, or ecclesiastical purposes is destined to meet with increasing opposition.

Apart from any appraisal of its strong or weak points UNESCO (United Nations Educational, Scientific and Cultural Organization) is an indicator of the opportunity for Christian education throughout the world. It symbolizes the recognition of a universal responsibility for the promotion of educational projects and opportunities which puts the Church in the educational field. In its origin it was intended to express and advance the new interest in education for all. At present, like the United Nations itself, this organization is in the experimental stage. How it develops will be largely determined by the kind of people who maintain an interest in it, a fact about all organizations which Christians often overlook.

The current significance of UNESCO for the Church centers in what it tells us about the widespread interest in education and the hopes which the common man entertains through the prospect of more education.

For Christian education UNESCO is not an instrument. It is a marker pointing to a door of opportunity through which the molder of the Christian way of life may achieve his goal if he will enter. It heralds abroad the fact that educational forces are at work influencing the life of the common man everywhere. It clearly challenges Christian education to take its place and to move with adequate resources and effective procedures if its way of life is to be stamped upon the character and personality of the millions who are now becoming intellectually emancipated.

CURRENT DISAPPOINTMENT AND ITS CAUSES

The realist, however, is likely to remind us that our optimism concerning the possibilities of Christian change through education should be tempered by a frank facing of its accomplishments thus far. In spite of the expansion of educational activity and the increase of knowledge, improvement in the quality of life has not showed a corresponding advance in the twentieth century. While the economic betterment in many areas of living can be attributed to the effect of education, it has not followed that in social, moral, and cultural relationships to know is to be. In fact the twentieth century has witnessed a deterioration of the moral, social, and cultural relationships within the educationally privileged classes. Education, we are reminded, did not stop a world war, nor did it prevent a world-wide economic depression. It has not eliminated juvenile delinquency, nor has it retarded the disintegration of family life. It has not cleaned away social and personal vulgarities, nor has it saved the individual from the self-destroying effects of moral deterioration.

While all of this must be acknowledged about life today, education must not be charged with the full blame. Rather, an examination of education should undertake to point out the areas of its responsibility and the places and causes of its failure within those areas. We must not permit education to be put in the untenable position of a cure-all, nor can we allow it to become the whipping boy for all the failures of our current society.

Where education has fallen short of its expectations, optimism about its future influence is justified by the fact that there have been reasons for its failures which can be overcome by education itself or by rectifying the faulty contributing factors of which education is only one.

With characteristic American overenthusiasm we have expected education in and of itself to do too much. We have looked to it as the dominating factor in transforming the individual and in remaking society. But education has never really had that power, nor has it actually occupied that position. It will always fail our expectations when it is given the full task of developing a person to the place where he will make responsible decisions about life. Without education at its best man can never experience the realization of his best. Nevertheless, with only knowledge and skills to turn to, life always falls below its capacity for betterment. Education alone cannot save the world, and it should not be expected to. But without education for all, the world cannot be saved.

Education has not produced the results in good living expected of it because of its tendency to overemphasis. Always susceptible to fads, education can easily lose a balanced point of view in its philosophy and method. Coming on a discovery, it has been inclined to overdo it to the neglect of other already established factors in the success of the educational process. In the molding of character what a person should do and why he should do it are as important as how things should be done. But modern education in a marvelous age of technical invention and discovery has equipped us with the skills of living without giving those who have acquired the power to do a compelling reason for doing and a personal commitment to live by these reasons.

Education has also been handicapped in what it can do for man by the attitudes which man has had toward education. When education is looked on as an end in itself rather than a means for improving the quality and enlarging the capacity of life, it will always be disappointing. Understanding and applying the uses of education are as important as acquiring it. The quantitative standards of American education have tended to distract our thought from its primary importance, which is measured by how much knowledge we have acquired, how we think of its uses, and the skill we have in applying our education to its intended uses. The minimum number of years one must spend in school before he can secure a work certificate has a legitimate educational purpose which the quantitative requirement of so many years in school cannot by itself accomplish. The purpose on its highest level is to make the growing citizen a good and competent one. But simply putting in a given number of school years does not produce such a citizen as experience points out. The knowledge he has acquired, the intentions he has developed, and the skill he possesses to unite knowledge and intention determine the prospects for his future. The same can be said for the attainment of a college degree as the password at the door of social acceptability and commercial opportunity. An old Indian chief had a point for important consideration in the evaluation of a college education when he observed that he had been through many colleges, but no college had been through him.

The educational system tends to fix the idea that education is an end in itself by its quantitative standards for professional approval and advancement. No one having been associated with the schools would discount the importance of formal education for those who teach. Nevertheless, something very essential in good teaching is lost when the necessity of having an advanced degree as a badge of attainment overshadows the consideration of what the teacher actually knows, his philosophy of life, his experience with life, and the influence of his example and teaching upon the student. The product rather than the leader's personal attainments determines the effectiveness of education.

This attitude of looking upon education as an end in itself has been one of the causes for the disappointing results in some of our Christian education. Perfect attendance records in the church schools, catechism and Bible memory work, and more time for study are all to be encouraged. As yet we have not met the minimum uses for these means of Christian education, to say nothing of the maximum. However, what a pupil learns and what he learns to do with what he learns are the real assurances for an indelible imprint of the Christian way of life upon his character. Awareness as to why we have religious education and of what we are to do with it opens the channels for its effective use. Selection of what to learn can offset the reduced time available for Christian education in our modern life. The development of attitudes toward life gives the degree of value to all that is learned.

Often education's power is weakened by man's uncritical attitude toward it. The world passed through an era when it believed that education could do no wrong. Anything that attached to it the name of education was good. And we are still under the influence of this attitude even though the evidences of its destructive consequences are painfully apparent. All education, either secular or Christian, is not good, even though it may be both efficient and modern. Hitler's education for German youth was certainly efficient. It was modern in its repudiation of the time-tested moral maxims of life, and it was progressive in the unrestrained expressional side of certain youth relations. It worked, but its product was destruction.

Educators and those to be educated often make the mistake of looking on new methods as final rather than experimental. So they throw out the old before the new has a chance to prove itself, only to discover, after the damage is done, that it doesn't work and the pupil pays for it. We seek to overcome one evil and lose sight of the other evils which our new methods often create. Making education interesting and easy are commendable objectives, but when the process produces ignorance as it has in the field of English and mathematics and in the content of religious education, it becomes both harmful and demoralizing.

The methods of education are not sacrosanct. Neither is novelty the measure of sound practice. "Test everything" and cleave to that which actually produces life-improving results is the test which makes education an instrument for betterment.

The growing feeling that the state should provide more bountifully for education than it has in the past presents this age with the temptation to judge educational effectiveness in terms of its physical equipment. More schools and better school buildings are greatly needed, and good equipment can be an instrument for better teaching. However, their value is determined by their use. It is what takes place within the school and its environs which actually makes the lasting imprint upon the life of the pupil. This observation seems so obvious that it would hardly appear necessary to record it. Nevertheless, there are unmistakable evidences that some educators and many to be educated are not seeing this relationship in its true perspective. In securing the better equipment needed, there is a tendency in some quarters to assume that a good product will be insured. These tangible things which can be seen and can make a striking impression can distract one's consideration from the really determinative factors in the outcome of education. A beautiful campus is no substitute for a poor faculty, and cathedrallike public schools are a pretense for good education if the teachers treat their work as "hewers of wood and drawers of water" (Josh. 9:21). A teacher with character, personality, and a sound philosophy of life can use effectively good equipment; but good equipment cannot substitute for a teacher of negative character, indifferent personality, and a questionable philosophy of life. Regardless of what you surround a pupil with, unless he understands the real purpose of education and has a will to achieve it, nothing very improving will happen to him because of his educational experience. What is taught and who teaches determine the contribution which the physical equipment of education can make to the pupil.

Who teaches our youth, therefore, is the most important consideration in education. Yet so often in public school, church school, and college this question becomes a minor one in popular evaluation and choice. The kneeside teaching of a Susannah Wesley, the questions of a Socrates, the log method of a Hopkins, and the shade-tree school of a Tagore must not be excluded in the modern setting of education if the good life is to be education's goal.

Modern education is further handicapped in its service to the individual and to society by an attitude which would make it a substitute for religion. This conception of education leaves the impression that religion is a nonessential if not an actual deterrent to the emancipated. It has offered a self-created faith in science and technology as the guarantee for improvement in a world which is to be thought of as man-made and not God-created. Paul as an educator dealt with it in his day, calling it a vanity of the mind which darkens the understanding and alienates man from the life of God by ignorance and through the hardening of the heart (Eph. 4:17-18). Neglecting the development and training of the determinative factor in a person's life, which is his spirit, education may still bring man possessions and accomplishments, but not the power or wisdom to safeguard their preservation and insure their constructive uses. Here lies the crux

70

of man's current personal and world problem. This theory of education, which eliminates the supernatural in man and the religious element in his education, has made the mistake of identifying virtue with knowledge. It has created the false assumption that the more education one has, the less religion he needs. It has damaged man's confidence in victory through allegiance to God and compensated for it with a grim determination to keep one jump ahead of disaster. Thus it makes of the best-trained and most widely educated generation a groping, uncertain, confused, and purposeless mob.

Education must never be though of as a substitute. It replaces no normal function or need in human life. Applied to all of life it enriches and empowers. Alone it can do very little. The restoration of religion's gate pass to many of our college campuses and the return of theology as a part of liberal and general learning are indications of a much-more-realistic view of an education for all of life.

THE CHRISTIAN CRITICISM OF EDUCATION

What we are facing in regard to education's possibilities and failures, Jesus dealt with in his generation; and what he said is pertinent for our times.

Jesus found education ailing in its purpose. To him what the educated people of his day did not know was not as serious as their lack of comprehension concerning the uses of their learning. He accused them of throwing away the "key of knowledge" (Luke 11:52). They did not enter into the larger life it made possible; and by their example they prevented others, looking to them for leadership, from entering in.

The key which opened the door of usefulness for education in the Master Teacher's judgment was the conception of its purpose. What it was supposed to do and how it was to be used to accomplish its most desirable ends were the facts which when ignored or misunderstood kept the doors to the larger and better life closed.

To the question "Why, knowing so much, do we not live better?" Christian criticism replies in the Master's language. We have lost the key which unlocks and releases our possessions in education for our salvation. We are unmindful of educational values. We are blinded to education's real purpose. We are both accumulating and freezing educational assets. We have not opened the doors which will release them for work.

The key to power through education is purpose. After we have acquired an education, there will be disappointing results unless we clearly understand what it is intended to do.

On the lower levels and for its secondary uses the educational function is widely understood in modern life. It is being used effectively in creating the facilities for living. It has increased the goods which make living easier and more comfortable. Whether or not it has increased the enjoyment of living is a debatable question, but it has certainly multiplied the entertainment for life. Christianity recognizes all these uses of education as legitimate. It has no quarrel with education which creates better physical and material conditions for living. It says, however, that these are not enough, nor are they of first importance. It asks that they be given their proper place, which is secondary, and that they may not be permitted to blot out or supplant the real objectives of the acquisition of knowledge. Christianity insists that we must be forever learning and that we must also come to a knowledge of the truth about ourselves and our world. This, Christianity holds, is the responsible function of education on all levels and in all its manifestations. And to do this education must recognize man's spiritual origin and destiny and make its contribution to the understanding of our supernatural origin and to the achievement of our spiritual destiny. It challenges a theory of education which denies this function, and it charges education with the responsibility for clarifying man's spiritual relationships and maintaining them in a secularistic society.

THE CHRISTIAN PURPOSE IN EDUCATION

Supported by Jesus' teaching and example and validated by human experience, the Christian philosophy of education can claim three sharply defined purposes. They are plain enough for all who are involved in either giving or receiving an education to understand, and they are profound enough to require the most serious attention to the methods which education must employ for their realization.

First, Christianity holds that the intellectual purpose of education is to dispel ignorance. From the beginning of human life on this planet until now people and their civilization have been "destroyed for lack of knowledge" (Hos. 4:6). The extent of this destruction has been multiplied where power and zeal have not been accompanied by a corresponding increase in knowledge. There is no place in the modern world for ignorance. The informed mind is the prerequisite to the improved life.

The ignorance, however, which must be dispelled is not always fully comprehended. It is of two kinds. The first is the ignorance of facts. A body of knowledge is required to preserve, improve, and expand life. Since there is so much that mankind around the world does not know, education is largely concerned with providing people with facts. The know-how of life is a necessity for survival. This kind of education is by nature quantitative. It is the manual-dictionary-encyclopedia type of learning. It is the first to be provided, the easiest to acquire, and too often it constitutes the only incentive to learn.

In its most effective form factual education involves three processes: assembling, analysis, and organization of the facts. There is some complaint that our educational system is not doing as good a job as it should in dispelling factual ignorance either by a selection of essential facts to be learned or by their acquisition

73

and organization for use. We hear of college graduates ignorant of the essential facts in the common branches of knowledge. They cannot spell or write a sentence or add a column of figures. Popular surveys report an amazing ignorance of the facts of history, religion, and politics. Real craftsmen are, we are told, becoming fewer. Many skills are passing into the category of lost arts. And a "workman who has no need to be ashamed" (II Tim. 2:15) seems not to be the chief objective of the trades. The idea of giving a person a specific body of knowledge to live with has been superseded by a splash theory of the acquisition of knowledge which assumes that, when one is exposed to the facts of life, the essential adheres. There is some truth in all such criticisms. But after the admittance of the deficiencies of modern education in its activities to dispel the ignorance of facts, the truth remains that factually we of this generation know much more about the world, ourselves, and one another than any of our predecessors. Certainly the availability of factual knowledge is at the fingertips of all who will reach out for it. And what has been accomplished in improving the processes required for better living by the possession of such knowledge is highly creditable.

Why, then, is there so much pessimism about the future and so great uncertainty in dealing with the distressing situations of the present? Why is the twentieth century called the Age of the Cassandras? People in possession of much knowledge, but who see life deteriorate before their very eyes, feel helpless in their efforts to stop the downward trend.

The reason for this sense of frustration and ineptitude is to be found in modern man's failure to dispel the second kind of ignorance—the ignorance of the meaning and significance of the facts which have been accumulated. It is the failure which comes when people are ever learning but never coming to the knowledge of the truth. Having the facts, modern man does not know what to do with them or what to make them do for him. Here is the most destructive lag in the dissipation of human ignorance.

To the knowledge of what facts mean and what they portend, this age as a determinative group has lost the key. We possess the facts, but we do not understand the language through which they seek to speak to us. We have taught ourselves to learn, but not to think. We gather, we analyze, we organize, but we do not generalize. We do not reach conclusions. We are historians seeing clearly the past but not prophets possessing the long view of the future. We evolve from all our fact gathering no clear and confident policy for planning life's tomorrows.

This is the kind of ignorance which is the roadblock to progress in the modern world. It has deadened the twentieth century to the evil ways of living which have entrenched themselves only because we would not listen to what the facts available were telling us about the inevitable outcome of these evil ways. It has caused the age which knows the most to repeat its mistakes over and over again. We are not failing for a lack of experiences from which to draw a conclusion, but because we are not teaching people how to read meaning in the facts abundantly available. This accounts for the increasing personal disintegration within the higher social, economic, and intellectual levels of society. It explains, at least, how people with a high degree of literacy can be completely deceived as to the nature and outcome of the totalitarian philosophies.

So the most serious intellectual concern of contemporary education is not the spread of technical or utilitarian knowledge. People sense a need for this and will have it. Man's intellectual undoing, the reason for his tragic and colossal failures in bringing the good life to himself and to his social order, lies in his inability to draw lessons fom experiences, to discern values in facts, to develop standards from experimentation, and to project the present into the future by means of reflection and ordered imagination. Thus he faces the situations of life unprepared. The facts get through their meaning to him too indistinctly and too late. He becomes a prey to the passing influence, good or bad, because he lacks this power of discernment.

Now the intellectual purpose of education must aim at the rectification of this deficiency in judgment, evaluation, and meaning. It must face the task of developing the desire and the power to think upon the knowledge and experience of life within a generation which has discounted and neglected this kind of education. It must re-emphasize a phase of education which our fathers called liberal because it fitted a free man for living and which has largely dropped out of a free man's preparation for living in a world where his way of life is challenged. In short, wisdom as well as knowledge must be its goal.

On the higher levels an adequate program of education which will dispel the widespread ignorance of significance, value, and meaning of our accumulated knowledge and experience must come for the professional educators. The man in the street can do little more than to challenge them to find the way to dispel this blighting kind of ignorance. But when it dawns upon the rank and file that they are being constantly taken in because they cannot read the score or will not face the necessity of learning how to sense what is taking place, we can then expect gains in living to be made and to be retained. Awareness to this condition is, therefore, the first step in its rectification.

Religious education has a positive as well as a supplemental contribution to make in the development of the faculty of judgment and evaluation. Values, standards, and meaning have always been the concern of religion. Its textbook, the Bible, is a series of events taking place within the framework of history, teaching man a lesson about himself and his future. It has dealt with the art of living rather than with the skills of a livelihood. It has emphasized the importance of right attitudes, genuine values, and specific standards. It has given man a reason for living and an explanation of life.

So in dispelling ignorance, education cannot realize its intellectual purpose without the inclusion of religious education on its instructional team. Religion is the doorway through which man passes to an adequate meaning of life. Through it he acquires a pattern of thought which enables him to discern between good and evil, true and false, permanent and transitory. And without the ability to draw conclusions on which to base actions the chances for the Christian imprint are dangerously lessened.

In the second place, Christianity contends that education must have a moral purpose if it is to leave a Christian imprint upon personality and character. "Truth for truth's sake" has its aesthetic justification; but if the incentive for acquiring truth and an understanding of its uses do not transcend its intrinsic value, little will be accomplished by it in developing, expanding, and insuring the better life. The use of knowledge for the good life requires it to be channeled through a moral purpose to fight evil and to correct error.

To begin with, all learning is intended to teach the difference between right and wrong, good and bad, the helpful and the destructive, the valuable and the worthless. A well-educated person is equipped by his education to make these distinctions on the basis of experience and judgment. He should know enough to avoid the messes of life concerning which there is guidance in past human experiences and also to detect current and future pitfalls by applying to his choices the standards for assaying them which his education has supplied.

The good uses of all other knowledge depend upon the knowledge which reveals moral worth. We are indebted to Plato for pointing this relationship out to us. "Without the knowledge of good and evil," he said, "the use and excellence of the sciences will fail us." How much to validate his observation has come within the actual experience of the twentieth century.

However, the force and lifting power of education have been seriously inactivated by an enervating indifference to its moral imperatives. Thought and action have been kept apart by a theory of education which detached the acquisition of knowledge from its compulsion. The whole scene of life in the Western world is being affected by the resulting agnostician. We suffer from an anomalous situation where people equipped with knowledge either feel no obligation to act upon their knowledge or have not been taught how to reach clear-cut decisions by means of that knowledge. The people of the Western world resemble the Ephraimites, who "armed with the bow, turned back on the day of battle" (Ps. 78:9). We have trouble deciding what to do; and having reached a decision, we falter in carrying it out to its logical and ultimate realization.

It is fanciful to expect the triumph of the Christian way of life by assuming that truth can be neutral in the moral decisions which life requires or that a detached indifference to the down-to-earth struggles for the maintenance of Christian standards is the mark of a truly educated person. Neutrality regarding the uses of truth is a contradiction of terms. Such neutrality is in its effect opposition. It abets the destroyers of truth. Likewise the social and personal values of knowledge are effective only when applied to the daily life we live.

The gap between thought and action is a serious obstacle confronting the free world in maintaining its own life and in making it available for others. Bridging that gap so that those who know what to do will proceed to do it is a responsibility which the society of a free world rightly places upon both education and religion. Now to make action the compulsion of thought, knowledge and commitment must be considered parts of a total process. They cannot be separated if what education teaches becomes what men live by. Likewise education and evangelism must form a new working alliance, each understanding the function of the other and each recognizing its need of the other. The once-popular assumption that education and evangelism are totally separate operations in the development of life has been thoroughly repudiated by the results of this separation. Religious education made this mistake as well as secular education. Now from such responsible bodies as the American Council on Education we are warned that "it is the business of public education to impel the young toward a vigorous decisive personal reaction to the challenge of religion."

The good life depends ultimately upon moral patriotism. Great teaching not only inspires the search for truth but also quickens the application of it to life. Here is where both democracy and Christianity have failed. Scholarship has not been touched with the fire of moral patriotism. We have the power of knowledge, but we lack the power of moral compulsion.

[The danger, therefore], for educated people in the democratic countries is not too few but too many opinions; not to be pinned in a single belief, but to be puzzled by innumerable alternatives; not a closed mind, but an irresolute one; to drift unanchored from deeps to shallows; from safe water to the rocks; an incapacity to refuse evil and choose the good. A major task of education is to help to the right choice.[1]

The Christian position requires education to have a spiritual purpose. While the humanistic and utilitarian aspects of education are important, the total purpose of education must be more than humanistic and utilitarian, the man-made ways of attaining a career. Knowing the ways of living and using them to improve the conditions of life and increase the standards of consumption leave man with an incompleteness which cannot be satisfied apart from the consideration of his destiny. Man to be complete must know where he is going, why he must go in that direction, and how to arrive at his destination. Unless his education enables him to evolve satisfying answers to these questions, he will become an immature and insecure person. Such is the situation for multi-

[1] Livingstone, *op. cit.* Used by permission of Cambridge University Press.

tudes today who have had more than the average education. In fact the greater the amount of knowledge, as education today provides it, the more inscrutable the worthwhileness and destiny of life seem to become. The attempts to put purpose and meaning into human life on the basis of adjustment to the conditions of life or self-interest for survival or by accommodations which result in compromises for immediate gains have all proved inadequate to say the least. The interpretation of life which begins with the biological fact of birth and ends with the physical fact of death has not provided a sufficient impulse for sustained altruism under continuous assault. The solely humanistic interpretation of life has made modern man a frustrated, uncertain, and inept person.

But Christianity holds that man does not need to be this type of person even in the midst of adverse conditions of living. It insists that the correction of this self-destroying outlook upon life is both possible and necessary. It further holds that the remedy must come through the right kind of education and that education brings a wholeness and assurance to life when it prepares man for his destiny by a consideration of the more-than-humanistic aspects of his being. Human destiny must be understood in the light of God's purpose. It deals with man's supernatural origin, God's plan for the world, and man's life in this world and the world to come. Education for all of life must relate man understandingly and usefully to a transcendent order beyond persons and their immediate needs and desires. It must educate man as a spiritual being as well as a social animal. And it must acknowledge the creative aspects of man's spirit as well as its expressional forms.

It is for these reasons that a Christian philosophy of education insists that all education must have an adequate spiritual purpose. This constitutes education's third service to the life of man.

Clarity and precision must characterize the discussion of a spiritual point of view in education lest its genuineness be lost in a kind of professional double talk which uses a spiritual vocabulary and attaches to it only humanistic meanings. It makes a great difference whether, when we use such terms as "standards," "values," "faith," and "order," we mean what man himself creates by accommodation and convenience or what has been "destined before the foundation of the world" (I Pet. 1:20). God, for instance, conceived and offered as the accumulation of human values bears a quite different relationship to man's destiny and its achievement than God who means to man the Father of our Lord and Saviour Jesus Christ.

As the point of spiritual purpose in education a clarification between a humanistic and a theistic interpretation is greatly needed. This differentiation perhaps can best be achieved for the rank and file of those who are to be educated by a simple and unequivocal statement of the meaning of spiritual purpose. This is the function of its religious guardians and interpreters, the exponents of the Christian faith.

In its plainest terms Christianity holds that the spiritual purpose of education is to exalt God. By whatever methodology education uses, the result must not be the ensmallment of God in the mind and life of the educated. Christianity bases this conception of education's spiritual purpose on an interpretation of the meaning of life and justifies it by the tragic results to man and his world when trained to live by the self-destroying illusion of atheism.

To the ever-recurring words of the Psalmist "Thou dost show me the path of life," Jesus voiced agreement when for himself he acknowledged that life begins in God and goes to God. "This," he said, "is life eternal that they might know the only true God." When the possession of eternal life is thought of as the gift of God, it produces quite a different effect upon all that a person becomes than a conception of life which sets man up as both its architect and builder. The Christian permits a fading or a distorting of the spiritual purpose of education at the peril not only of blocking a Christian society but of destroying the good life within himself.

Human experience likewise supports the Christian interpretation of an adequate spiritual purpose in education since the major self-destroying illusions of modern society have sprung from a denial of a personal God active in the life of man. All forms of social and political totalitarianism have gained control of man by first destroying his belief in a Christian God. Facism reverted to paganism for its conception of religion. It controlled its citizens, not by denying God, but by making him a lesser loyalty among the many state duties it bound upon the life of its citizens. Communism banished God until it destroyed the confidence of the people in his supremacy and moral finality and then tolerated his return on a basis of restricted activity confined to the insignificant areas of human life. Secularism reversed the positions of man and God, deluding the created to believe that he was greater than the Creator and to consult, therefore, with himself rather than with God in making life's decisions. By the flattery of thinking of (themselves) more highly than they ought (Rom. 12:3), the people of the twentieth century have been induced to surrender their spiritual purpose, believing that thereby they could attain freedom from personal responsibility. Now it is dawning upon them that their license has brought them to a slavery of both body and soul. Seeking liberty "they themselves are slaves of corruption" (II Pet. 2:19).

Bringing God out of exile and putting him back upon the throne of all life is the real issue before the nations of the world today; and in planning the strategy for the return of God, we must not ignore the major role which education played in his overthrow. When the necessity and the power to think for oneself, and the moral responsibility to act upon conclusions, and the destiny of man attained through intellectual and spiritual fellowship with the God revealed in Christ, were removed as the chief objectives of education, the molds of life lost their

Christian imprint, man lost the power of Christ's transforming touch, and society lost the sources for its inner improvement.

Many useful functions were, of course, substituted by education for those which were put aside; but the educated have faced a world of challenge without a sense of rights or their value and with an attitude which binds them to the lower instead of lifting them to the higher.

New sights in all education are imperative. A change of direction involving a change of heart as well as curriculum is required to acquaint life with its larger meanings. In short the Christian philosophy of life is alone adequate for an education of man's mind, his will, and his spirit if he is to preserve his heritage and achieve his destiny in an age which is destroying the one and ignoring the other. "For whatever the world thinks, he who hath not much meditated upon God, the human mind and the *summum bonum*, may possibly make a thriving earthworm, but will certainly make a sorry patriot and a sorry statesman." [2]

Here Christians must take their stand, demanding for their young the conditions of nurture which will create a spiritual atmosphere for their development, supplying it by their own interest and example, and teaching it in systems of education, both secular and religious, which are committed to the spiritual philosophy of life.

[2] George Berkeley, *Siris*.

CHAPTER IV

THE CHRISTIAN CONTENT

Jesus increased in wisdom and in stature,
and in favor with God and man.
—LUKE 2:52

IN THE WORLD TODAY WE MEET MANY PEOPLE WHO NO LONGER live by the pattern of life to which they were molded in their younger years. They do not adhere to its social forms, neither do they observe its religious customs. They have in varying degrees discarded its morality and show a dullness to its principles in decision and action. The pattern which the guiding hand of earlier influence in home, church, school, and community thought it had indelibly impressed has shown an alarming tendency toward losing its sharp lines of distinction. Much of it is being rubbed off by contact with the abrasive social customs of the world. Its luster has become dim. The form shows disfiguration through abuse. Where some evidences of the pattern once impressed still persist, they remain in the lives of many as the vestige of habit rather than the expression of principle.

When you talk to these people, they will tell you that they once lived like you do, believed as you believe, and practiced your customs of life. They observed the Christian social and personal disciplines. They lived by the so-called "holy habits." They learned the rules by heart and can still quote the Bible and the catechism. But times changed, and they changed with the times. And the persons they once were they no longer are.

Many parents, seeing what the acids of modernity are doing to the pattern they thought they had imprinted on the lives of their children, are both baffled and distressed by the changes they observe. They cannot account for the easy acceptance of the vulgarities, the lack of good taste, and the adulteration of refinement in the present styles of living. They worry about the crumbling of moral resistance to the onset of non-Christian practices. They are shocked by the intellectual defiance to age-old axioms. Furthermore, they feel helpless in going about the restoration of the imprint they thought was permanent. "What can we do?" they ask. "We tried to bring our children up right." So they turn to the church, the school, and the community with the question, "Cannot you do something about it?"

Of course these institutions can do something to sharpen and strengthen the Christian imprint provided they have the intelligent and persistent co-operation of all who in some way have a part in the process.

To start with, something must be done to dispel the hysteria of helplessness which has gripped the character-making forces. To wring one's hands in despair and condemn the inadequacies of the fire-fighting forces is no way to save the contents of a burning house. And to stand by in helpless disorganization while the forces which would destroy the Christian imprint upon life are at work invites total disaster. Too many good people have the notion that nothing really significant can be done to impress, protect, and maintain the Christian imprint upon personality, conduct, and character under present conditions. So with an attitude of defeat a compromise of the Christian position appears to be a victory. The invasion of impressionable areas by non-Christian practices without a struggle to keep them free from such contamination has rendered the Christian task much more difficult. Retreat from the full Christian position under the onslaught of popular pagan and evil pressures has also damaged the advantages of prestige for the Christian way of life and belief in its superior power.

Therefore, the first task of the forces undertaking to insure the dominance and the permanence of the Christian imprint is to restore sense and order to the panic-stricken forces which have been experiencing only defeat for their efforts.

The present campaign to remove the Christian imprint loses some of its bullying ruthlessness when seen as something old rather than as something new. The molders of the Christian imprint have had a long experience in dealing with it. It is not a phenomenon of modern living for which no antidotes have been developed and no cures as yet found.

The problem of living a godly life in a godless world is as old as life itself. The three Hebrew young men taken to the pagan court of Nebuchadnezzar had the imprint of their early life put to the test, a most severe test in fact, involving conviction, risk, and resistance and calling for faith and courage. The imprint held up. It was neither dulled nor removed, and the young men won a victory and enjoyed the fruits of that victory.

The conflict of imprint with environment constitutes the plot in the Sodom story of Lot and his wife, developing the lines of triumph for one and of defeat for the other.

The same situation confronted the parents of Jesus when they were compelled to take their infant Son to Egypt. There in the most impressionable period of his life, while the religious imprint was forming, it was confronted with the infiltration of pagan surroundings. Only within the four walls of his home was the little Jesus immune from the forces of an alien social and religious life. Outside the gods of his playmates were many and sensual. The ethics and morality of play were pagan. The education of the street was Egyptian not Hebrew. But the godly imprint formed and hardened in spite of the unfavorable conditions.

The letters of John Wesley to his mother, while he was at Cambridge, reveal the presence of the conflict in living then which confronts us now. His kind were few, and the other kind were many. His way was fighting for its place, and their way was established. How he could "live the Lord's life in a strange collegiate land" was the theme of many of the letters which he and his mother exchanged. And he found a way with dignity, honor, and reward to emerge with an imprint of life which supplanted its traducer.

A steady look at the facts of experience reveal the possibility of victory rather than the inevitability of defeat. Matched with the present the past appears even more vicious in its attacks upon the Christian imprint. Yet from its periods of unpopularity and submerging the Christian imprint emerged to enjoy wide and appreciative acceptability in the very places of its worst humiliations.

The past speaks a word of encouragement to the present in the effort to strengthen and to preserve the Christian imprint. It points up the fact that the Christian imprint has been able to survive the ravages of the most destructive and varied attacks. Provided the job of upbringing has been of the right sort, the past lends credence to the maxim:

> Train up a child in the way he should go,
> And even when he is old he will not depart from it.
> Prov. 22:6 (A.S.V.)

It challenges the present to fight rather than surrender. And it establishes the fact that what today may be a neglected and a clumsy art need not become a lost one.

THE PLACE AND NATURE OF CONTENT

Experience indicates that the operation is not a salvage process by which a new pattern of living would incorporate both Christian and pagan features. Nor is it to be found in the removal of Christian living from an atmosphere which is hard on it. Rather the situation calls for a better quality and fusing of the elements on which the imprint is formed, worked at more intelligently and consistently. Only by such methods can we hope to produce an imprint capable of resisting the strongest destructive forces.

This new element in the field of method has been called the "clue to Christian education" and is described as the discovery of the relation of doctrine to experience. It must be worked out in a more effective adjustment of content (what one believes) and method (how one expresses what he believes) in the development of the Christian way. Truth must become the motive of action if the imprint is to remain firm. But truth must first be known and understood before it can become the dominating motive in what man does. There is something in knowing what life is all about which stiffens and maintains a way of conduct. Much of the imprint smooths out because of a relaxing of internal pressures. Man decides it is not worth while, and then the Christian expression of life gives way. Only, therefore, when the imprint goes clear through life, reaching the depths of thought, coloring emotional responses, clarifying purpose, purifying motive, and solidifying conviction, can it be counted on to stand up under all conditions of living.

The new method, calling for a realignment of content with method, doctrine with experience, and truth to life, involves the question of what we teach people to believe as well as how we teach people to act. What goes into the making of life is more determinative of the outcome than what surrounds that life. The observation of the captain who brought his ship to port in a storm which took a complete toll of other craft in the path of its fury that it was not his expert seamanship, nor the abatement of the storm, in the final analysis which kept his ship afloat, but it was what went into its construction, is a modern parable of life in these times. Skill and surroundings are important factors in maintaining the Christian life; but what has gone into the making of that life, the quality of life itself, is the factor that really determines the outcome.

Therefore, if we want to produce a Christian imprint which will stand up, we must pay greater attention to the content of the life on which it is impressed, its quality, its depth, its purity, and its knowledge. Shoddy, shallow, contaminated, and uninformed persons are no base on which to put an enduring imprint of Christ's way of living.

A knowledge of the nature of the life to be imprinted and of the circumstances under which it must be lived is essential to the determination of the content to be put into life as well as the training for its expression. However, to quicken interest in the inwardness of living is not easy. There seems to be a natural resistance to a consideration of the deeper things of life, the sources out of which action springs. Many parents in their re-action to this type of education are like the mother who wrote to the teacher of her daughter's physiology class a note which said, "Don't teach Mary any more about her insides." Some of this hesitancy is understandable when you observe the wrong kind of teaching in this field and its morbid and erotic results in the pupil's life. Normal-living, healthy-minded, God-respecting teachers with much common sense and pedagogical skill are required for this work. It is a field where the amateur and the frustrated seeking compensations should be kept out.

Human life is different by nature and endowment from animal life. The Christian theory of creation points up the unique difference. One is natural, and the other is supernatural. One, therefore, has qualities and possibilities which the other can never possess. A chasm divides these two types of life which no amount of human ingenuity, training, or growth can bridge. The dimness of this distinction has been the cause of much poor quality in living. It makes a great difference whether a person thinks of himself as a little lower than the angels or just a little higher than the animals. You can train an animal until he develops a quick and clever response to certain outward stimuli, but the inward decisions which concern judgment, choice, and future actions and commitments an animal never makes. These inner reactions are distinctly human characteristics. But the personal equation bulks large in the kind of life a person develops for himself. The inward factors are the determining ones. Yet it is amazing how widely and popularly this distinction is overlooked in the educational processes on all levels of human development. It is denied in popular types of educational philosophy. A haziness in understanding this distinction is responsible for the breeding-stable pattern of child nurture where the emphasis is put upon the physical, social, and material aspects rather than upon the spiritual, personality, and character aspects of human development. Paradoxical as it may seem, inoculation against disease germs often carries the authority of law; but inoculation against diseased ideas is often condemned as an infringement on the right of self-expression. Beautiful physical surroundings are given more attention in many phases of education than the beauty and quality of associates in the educational experience. The log-cabin home of Abraham Lincoln would have been on the spot under the surveillance of many twentieth-century social-welfare organizations. The orphanage with less work hours, better physical surroundings and educational facilities, might have won in the argument. But the determinative factor in Lincoln's early life was Nancy Hanks. This illustration is not used to defend log cabins, but to lift to their proper place of importance the "Nancy Hanks" in developing the pattern and impressing the imprint of the good life.

Thus the content of what we teach must be based on this distinction if we intend to produce active and attractive Christians rather than healthy and successful pagans. You must

> Think on the seed ye spring from;
> Ye are made not to live life of brute beasts of the field.

Another factor which must be considered in the determination of what we teach our young is the status of the environment in which they are to live. They will always be confronted with the task of living the good life in an evil world. Environment can be improved, but except for its physical aspects its improvement in the twentieth century has been a disappointment to those who see it as a factor which should facilitate the living of the good life. The improvement of its economic aspects has not been accompanied by a corresponding reduction in its contributory relation to moral delinquency. Furthermore, a perfect environment would soon be corrupted unless perfect people lived in it. A better world is made by better people. Thus what we teach about the world and the life which must be lived in it has a major bearing on maintaining the imprint of the good life while living in that world. The problem is not to produce a life to be lived in a perfect world, but to develop a life which can express its highest qualities in an alien and hostile world.

Inherent quality will under these circumstances take precedence in the educational process over outward form, because it will be the quality of the inner life rather than the forms of conduct which will make and keep life good. We must, therefore, by carefully planned approaches quicken the development of quality living in the young, holding before them the "enduring vision of excellence," as Whitehead admonishes, and associating quality with the personal attributes of wisdom, courage, temperance, justice, intelligence, moral insight, liberality, high-mindedness, right ambition, good temper, friendliness, truth, just resentment, modesty, and decent respect for God and man. Think of what would happen if these quality marks of life which constitute the Greek-Judaic-Christian heritage were practiced before and taught to the rising generation. The inner pressures of such a life would insure the practice of good habits in spite of the corrosion of a contaminating environment.

One of the weaknesses of current life is its lack of conviction and its attitude that nothing matters enough to be maintained at all costs. This the Communists have discovered is the chief point of vulnerability in what they call the decadent West. It is a state of mind which has advocated retreat before every attack upon the moral and spiritual life of Christianity and the political life of democracy. No one seriously doubts the ability to take a stand and keep it, but every serious-minded person knows that somewhere in the development of the life of today the element which gives it a temper, that is, a hardness, the quality of resistance, has been left out. Man today could maintain the good life. He doesn't because he lacks the temper of worth-while purpose, of adequate meaning, of moral indignation, and of inner unity. Therefore, in the content of life Christian education must replace this missing quality if the Christian imprint is to survive and to multiply. We must find and implant the unifying element in life which impels man to know the truth and to make what is beautiful, to endure pain and fear, and to resist the allurement of pleasure on behalf of truth and goodness, and to serve society, not according to one's inclination, but in the measure of what is due.

All the world's great personalities have been conscious of this need. Plato called it the idea of the good. Confucius sought it in a "connecting string for all his knowledge." Paul found it in a Person in whom "all things hold together." A new school of thought in higher education is challenging all education to work for an "intellectual synthesis which must seek its unity in a theological basis." And William Temple gathered up this "temper of life" sought by great minds and needed by all as "trust in God." That in the experience of this schoolman and religious leader is the "Rosetta stone" which explains the otherwise futile and meaningless riddle of human existence. It is the missing element in the type who, "well-educated in the conventional sense, has no clear philosophy of life, nothing to fall back upon in the hour of stress, discouragement or indolence that all men experience, who is easily swept off his feet by current sophistries, or the fashion of the hour, and the voyage of whose life, even if he escapes these, tends to be 'bound in the shallows.' " [1]

THE CHRISTIAN CONTENT

A new consideration of what goes into the life on which the Christian imprint is to be impressed is a clear challenge to all who believe that the Christian imprint holds the way of the good life. The frank admission of the neglect of all education to this phase of human development is essential to its replacement. Likewise a serious examination of what is the right content to insure the fineness and permanence of the imprint is the first step in its restoration.

If we use the life of Jesus as a model, we discover four areas which must have spiritual content if they are to express the Christian imprint. Jesus, we are told, grew in wisdom and in stature and in favor with God and man. The Christian imprint in his life took four distinctive lines which related to body, mind, spirit, society. A Christian conception of each of these phases of living has been either nonexistent or inadequate in the personality patterns and their motivation produced by the education of this century. A Christian evaluation of them for purposes of daily living is basic to the preservation and extension of the Christian imprint upon life.

THE CHRISTIAN DOCTRINE OF THE BODY

Whitehead in his lectures to teachers said that "in teaching you will come to grief as soon as you forget that your pupils have bodies." [2] This observation is especially true of Christian teaching and the effort to give life the Christian imprint. To ignore the body and its relation to the other phases of a person's

[1] Livingstone, *op. cit.* Used by permission of Cambridge University Press.
[2] *The Aims of Education* (New American Library of World Literature).

life or to treat the body as an inferior vessel, troublesome and questionable in the expression of its function, has been a weakness in much of our recent religious education. It has too often resulted in no education or wrong education so far as the bodily functions are concerned. It has, in fact, turned the seeker for a healthy and livable doctrine of the body to the inadequate and destructive answers which have gained currency in recent decades.

The present age is body conscious. It spends vast sums to beautify, strengthen, and keep the body young. Mr. America is judged in terms of muscle, and the girls not to be outdone now have a nationally publicized contest to choose Miss Muscle Beach. The body gets more attention and creates more than any other element in human life.

What then has Christianity to say to the people of this generation about their bodies? What are they to be taught? How are they to think of their bodies, and what are the Christian uses to which the body is to be put? Is there a distinctive Christian doctrine of the body? If so, what is the content of that knowledge and how in normal, healthful, and practical ways can it be made to serve the fuller, happier purposes of life?

These are questions which have to be faced and effectively answered or we lose the battle for the Christian imprint before we begin. Youth and age, acutely conscious of their bodies, will find a philosophy to determine the bodily function; and much of the trouble within a person and in his social relations grows out of the fact that he has a tragically wrong conception of the relation of the body to the rest of his being and to the life of others.

Christian education will fail again in this phase of its task unless it faces sincerely its past failures and the present social frame in which it must prepare people to live with their bodies. Christian education has too often ignored this responsibility either because it was difficult or because of an archaic attitude on the part of people toward the discussion of the body in relation to life. Equally defeating has been an ivory-tower attitude in this phase of teaching which has divorced it from life and offered advice in terms of moral platitudes. Just as destructive has been a type of teaching so modernistic as to remove the Christian viewpoint, substituting for it prudential considerations which actually reduce the teaching to the pagan and naturalistic level.

Incompetent teachers have also contributed to the disregard or abortive uses of the Christian teaching about the body. The Church needs to be very wise in its selection of teachers and material in this field and very firm in keeping out the unworthy and the incompetent no matter how eager and sincere they may be. The task of teaching the teachers, be they parents, organization workers, school or social-agency representatives, or preachers, is the first step now demanding attention in preparing to give this generation some Christian content to their knowledge of and attitude toward their bodies. One sensible Christian living a normal and healthy life is worth as a teacher a multitude of theoretically trained, but neurotic (even slightly) and frustrated, individuals to whom such activities are really a compensation.

How people think of their bodies is basic to everything that they decide about their lives. A conception of what the human body is, as well as the uses to be made of it, releases or restricts the power to make all other phases of activity satisfying and life-giving.

Today the doctrine of the body and its uses most commonly held is a mixture of pagan desire and of Christian aught. At its lowest it emulates the ancient Roman attitude of sensationalism, which was sensual, sensuous, and physical, and evaluated its success upon its ability to produce the physical or sensate satisfactions. The commercialization of life has popularized this attitude toward the body. Advertising, current literature, the movies, all cater to this view as an effective allurement to purchase its wares. Romance in modern thinking has come to mean nothing more in popular thought than an experimentation in sex, and love becomes synonymous with physical attraction, and Christian morals are looked on as a dowdy attitude toward life dating its proponents to the Victorian age.

At its best the current doctrine of the body attaining social respectability resembles the Greek, which conceived the body as an instrument for the expression of beauty, intelligence, and of social and material achievement. Clean, strong bodies implemented healthy and able minds. Debauched bodies brought intellectual limitations and mental derangements. To the Greek the body at its best supremely expressed grace and charm, in contrast to the Roman, for whom the body at its best was judged by its physical allure. Bodily strength for the Greek was the medium through which social and material achievement had to pass. When, therefore, the medium was contaminated, the achievements were adulterated.

The Judaic-Christian doctrine of the body added a distinctly different conception to its philosophy and service. Whereas the Greek and Roman were essentially natural and physical in their conception of the bodily function, the Judaic-Christian explanation of the body was divine and spiritual. It made the body not only a vessel of use but also a vessel of honor. Recognizing its physical and instrumental services, the Judaic-Christian doctrine gave to their function a higher than human conception and motivation. Physical satisfaction had a social obligation and a divine function. Physical implementation was intended to do not only man's but God's work, permitting God in man to come to his most complete revelation and service in the world. The New Testament describes the body as God's house. He dwells in the human body and through it finds expression in life. "We are the temple of the living God," Paul said; and that is the motivation to "cleanse ourselves from every defilement of body and spirit."

(II Cor. 6:16–7:1.) The body is the home of the spirit of God I Cor. 3:16); therefore, it makes sense to teach that the "life of Jesus may also be manifested in our bodies" (II Cor. 4:10).

No Christian teaching is more plainly set forth in the Bible than that of the Christian meaning of the body and its functions as to origin, motivation, and expression. The modern sexologist is less successful in providing permanent satisfaction to man by his sex methodology than he is to incite sex experimentation. But the Bible teaches man how to live with his body all his life. It is in truth a very practical and up-to-date book on the physical relations of life. It cannot be superseded as a standard text on the subject. Perhaps more attention needs to be paid to an understanding rather than a circumvention of its teaching on this subject. Where, for instance, could a teacher of a group of young people find a better textual basis for the discussion of sex than in Paul's fourth chapter of First Thessalonians. In the modern language of J. B. Phillips every word is pertinent and sensible forming a basis for discussion rather than for argument.

Every one of you should learn to control his body, keeping it pure and treating it with respect, and never regarding it as an instrument of self-gratification, as do pagans with no knowledge of God. You cannot break this rule without in some way cheating your fellow-men. And you must remember that God will punish all who do offend in this matter, and we have warned you how we have seen this work out in our experience of life. The calling of God is not to impurity but to the most thorough purity, and anyone who makes light of the matter is not making light of a man's ruling but of God's command.[3]

The enlargement and application of this position would be a revelation of strength and beauty in sex to a host of modern youth whose approach to sex has been on the assumption that God had no word for them concerning it.

[3] *Op. cit.*

This in essence is the Christian doctrine of the body, and somewhere in the process of educational development it has dropped to a place of little or no consideration. It no longer is made the first thought of the child when the consciousness of his body dawns upon him. It is too often a pious or perfunctory consideration in the instruction given on sex relations. It is not the monitor it was intended to be in reminding us that bodily self-determination must take other than purely personal considerations into account. It is the forgotten lift needed to keep man erect when the physical allurements would reduce him to all fours. It is the one philosophy of the body which can, as Robert Hutchins says, "free man from the mammal within."

I submit the restoration of this point of view to dominant and understandable consideration as essential for the reclamation of a life-giving personal and social morality and for the return of human dignity to life in an age which has chained man to the lowest and robbed him of his self-respect.

We must face the fact that some traditional appeals for right physical relations no longer deter or persuade. Modern science has modified the physical penalties of moral wrongdoing. Scientific studies have not been of much help in moral improvement because they have been offered as substitutes for the religious point of view rather than supplements verifying religious assertions. An economic theory which magnifies indulgences as rights and shifts responsibility from the individual to society removes the prudential appeal based on the inevitable economic disaster which walks in the wake of wrongdoing. Such arguments are lightly brushed aside today. The fear of losing the necessities of life because of indulgence in excesses diminishes before the demand that the state regardless of a person's worthiness be responsible for supplying all with life's necessities. The war years which popularized the sanitation theory of morals and the biological theory of existence, confining life between the facts of physical birth and death, have made physical indulgences the criterion for many of life's desirabilities.

So the question "Do we have an effective instruction for the moral uses of the body?" must find its answer in a new approach, at least for this generation, which implants in the mind and imprints upon life's pattern the Christian view. People will have to begin thinking of themselves differently before their living will move to a higher level. And the new instruction must be directed to man at his best with no concession to the animal considerations which have brought him to his present low estate. The lines of the new view must be sharply drawn and made appealing and compelling. The Christian view of the body cannot retain for man everything the unchristian view now gives him, but it can offer him satisfaction on the above-animal level.

The change came for the better to the prodigal when he suddenly realized that he was the son of his father. King Henry made his punishment for the death of Thomas à Becket a personal triumph, maintaining his self-respect and dignity in the midst of his humiliation by insisting that, because he was a king, there should be no mitigation of the punishment for his wrongdoing. The difference came in his realization about himself. And the present generation, because it still has the divine instinct, can be counted on to respond to this higher view of life when it is presented as a release to something better and finer.

The corruption of Christian morals, the disintegration of the Christian home, and the contamination of Christian culture need purification at the source. The trouble is caused by how people really think of themselves. Specific personal problems such as sex, alcohol, and tobacco, as well as the social problems of home— divorce and human relations—need the soil of Christian reason to produce the fruitage of Christian forms.

Enslavement "to the elemental spirits of the universe" (Gal. 4:3) has little chance with a man who is conscious of the fact that he came from God and goes to God. Like Paul he faces the temptations of life with a determination not to be enslaved by anything. He has found a sufficient motivation, not only to keep his soul on top, but as a little girl misquoted it, "to keep his body under."

Somewhere, and mighty soon, society must come to grips with the whole field of moral delinquency or face its own destruction. Man cannot build a social paradise on the foundation of a barnyard morality. We haven't yet in the field of morals and social relations discovered how to reap what we do not sow. Nothing has ever been able to save a nation which flouted the lessons of past experience in moral standards or ignored the demands for their rewards. Yet the popular mind-set regarding morals is driving this age to make those disastrous mistakes. The wages of sin are death, and you don't change the pay by renaming the occupation.

It is certainly worth the attempt to imprint the lines of Christian morality in the current pattern of life by giving the person a Christian view of the body and its uses. To be sure, this effort will require long-term as well as short-term education; and its effects will be ultimate rather than immediate. But all other efforts having failed, the understanding and acceptance of the Christian meaning of physical life is society's last resort for its regeneration. The naturalistic conception of the body by itself leads to moral degeneration and social disintegration. Its place in Christian teaching is incidental to the Christian conception although in much of the sex instruction it has assumed a place of major attention. One's divine origin should be his first thought and not his afterthought in his physical and social adjustment to life. Thus the implanting of this view of the body must begin with the very young. The Christian teaching must come first. Like Manoah and his wife the parents who want their children to develop with a Christian view of their physical being and its relationships must send for the man of God to teach what the child's manner of life is to be. The first motivation should be goodness rather than strength or physical enjoyment or social approval. They follow when the higher view of life takes over. Physically destroying habits have a harder time getting a hold when the spiritual function of the body is clear in one's thinking. Good taste and morals have a spiritual origin and support. Human dignity has less to fear from the contamination of vulgar exhibitionism when a person thinks of himself as God's dwelling place. Men are harder to enslave when they consider themselves as a "little . . . lower than the angels" and "of more value than many sparrows." Life takes on a new carriage regardless of its social and material state when a man is conscious that God knows his name. Future homes build their security not in the sensate adjustments of physical accommodations, which are a changing relationship, but in a unity and a beauty which radiate from the God who set solitary people together in families and makes his dwelling place in their midst.

Life, thought of from its beginning and understood in each changing phase of human development in terms of this Christian view of the body and its functions, is the guarantee of a Christian morality which the corrosive pressures of environment cannot remove. Such a conception of the bodily function of life takes form and finds validation in minds which are the product of a Christian development.

THE CHRISTIAN DOCTRINE OF THE MIND

When Alexander the Great was about to embark upon his world conquests, Aristotle, his teacher, it is said, had a conversation with him concerning the effects of the outside world upon his life and thought. The teacher advised the pupil to be observing, alert, and aloof. He reminded Alexander that he was a Greek and must guard against the contaminating effects of the barbarian cultures upon his own mental processes. With this Alexander fully agreed. He did not want to lose his Greek point of view. But he also had realized that in the affairs of life a person cannot exist in a vacuum, nor can he live in an ivory tower. Man is a part of his environment either to change it or to be changed by it. And Alexander is reported to have replied to his teacher that, while he expected to preserve the Greek mind for himself, he looked on his mission as an opportunity to give the Greek mind to the rest of the world.

Since the purposes of Christianity can find fulfillment only in persons whose minds are conscious of their Christian function, the distinction which Alexander drew between an active and a passive attitude toward environmental influences must be borne in mind by those engaged in putting the Christian imprint permanently upon life. A mind passive to receive may change itself, but a mind active to give will change the world. For this reason a Christian doctrine of the mind becomes essential for all who would give a Christian imprint to the life they live.

That there has been neglect in clarifying and imparting a Christian conception of man's mind is evident in the current intellectual reactions to a philosophy of life and conduct. What people are doing and the reasons they give for doing it are windows through which the character of their mind is clearly revealed. Negative reactions to moral imperatives, social responsibilities, spiritual sensitivity, and to the refinements of personality indicate that the paganization of the Christian mind has taken the initiative away from the Christianization of the pagan mind. Public education according to Charles Clayton Morrison, the long-time editor of *The Christian Century*, presents the Church with a generation of youth whose minds have been set in the secular mold. The thought life of the United States shows alarming signs of deterioration when judged by Christian standards. And unless steps are taken early in life to safeguard the mind against these influences of deterioration, permanent rehabilitation, after the damage is done, becomes an impossible task.

How to develop and maintain a Christian mind is a subject about which there is great ignorance and sharp differences in practice and opinion. As compared with the attention paid to man's physical, social, and economic relations, the mind gets very little consideration from most people regarding its nurture, its nature, and its effect upon these other phases of living. Some adults act as if a mature Christian mind is simply the repetition of older persons' ways of thought and expression so that the young are not actually permitted to have or develop a mind of their own. Thus many adults remain intellectually immature and unsteady because of a "watch Papa" or "Mama knows best" misapplication to their thought development as children. Others come on disappointment by assuming that a knowledge of words indicates intellectual growth and power. Knowing the right answers is necessary knowledge, but it is no guarantee for right conduct or Christian judgments. "Knowledge is power" for good or ill according to its directives. Words and doctrines come alive only when they are expressed in actions. Others make no place for intellectual experimentation or on-the-spot decisions. By a casuistical approach they attempt to deal with problems on the hypothetical level before the facts in the individual case are known. It is like a layman treating disease from a home book on medicine. The situation is never exactly covered by the directions. Then theoretical knowledge never quite meets any actual life experience, since no two situations in life are ever just alike. A person well furnished with knowledge may fail miserably in Christian living because his mind has not been trained in judgment and discrimination and in the practical application of truth to life. This accounts for the prevalence of a type who mean well but always bungle, the persons with good ideas which they never seem to get into practice. It does not, however, justify the neglect and the subsequent tragic ignorance of Bible knowledge, religious history, and Christian philosophy which is an alarming characteristic of present-day education.

Now the practical questions for all who recognize the need for the Christian education of the mind are "What is a Christian mind?" and "How can it have an integral and sustaining effect upon life's Christian imprint?"

The first question finds its answer in Jesus, and the clue to the second comes from the experience of those who have sought successfully to let the mind of Christ dwell in them.

If Aristotle was correct in saying that the true nature of an organism is found in its highest development, then Jesus becomes the example, the demonstrator, and the transmitter of the Christian mind. We see it at its best in him. His intellectual life justified his invitation to "learn from me" (Matt. 11:29). We develop it within ourselves when we think his thoughts after him. A study of Jesus' mind is a prerequisite for producing the Christian imprint upon life. For conduct self-initiated is the projection of one's nature, and "as he thinketh in his heart, so is he" (Prov. 23:7 K.J.V.). How and what Jesus thought, why he thought as he did, and the ways he expressed his thought in life must be seriously studied if you are to "have this mind among yourselves, which you have in Christ Jesus" (Phil. 2:5).

Jesus' mental processes showed very definite characteristics which are capable of human approximation. Jesus had a developing mind. It did not "spring full-orbed" from the Godhead at his birth. Taking on himself the form of a man, he was subject to all the laws of human development; and this included a growing mentality. To say that Jesus was precocious and that his mental age was always considerably beyond his physical age, or that there was a divine element in his intellectual life, does not detract from the instruction lesser minds may find in a study of his mental processes. Jesus was more than superior mentally. He was divinely different with a uniqueness which man may approximate, but never attain, for himself. Nevertheless he is the prototype for a Christian mentality; and without the quality and character of Jesus' mind expressing itself in spirit and in conduct, the Christian imprint becomes an external form easily disfigured and rubbed away.

The distinctive aspects of Jesus' mind must, therefore, become clearly understood from the beginning if his mind is the type we develop in ourselves and our young.

Jesus' mind was a free mind. It belonged to him. The struggle for its possession recorded in the story of his life was not perfunctory. Jesus had to decide what he would let into his mind and to what and to whom he would give its highest allegiance. The assurance of all freedom and improvement in life lies in the realization that our minds belong to us and that what occupies them is controlled from within. This conception of the control of the mind is an attitude which must characterize a child's first thinking of himself and must be respected in the young by those who are older. When it is not inculcated early in life or is neglected in a child's education and its significance is not a conscious factor in life's decisions, the safeguard against all types of human enslavement is removed. For this reason totalitarianism fights to destroy this view of the mind's freedom, and true Christianity seeks to keep it alive.

Jesus had a growing mind. The incidents indicating this growth are recorded in the meager accounts of his life story. Beginning with the preparation of his mother and Joseph before his birth, it included lessons at his mother's knee, the discipline of his home, the training of the church school, the association of elders, worship in the synagogue, and a natural and avid curiosity about life which he put to good use in his teaching and counseling. Pride in bodily growth and in physical adornment and beauty is an established part of child education. Yet how infrequently is pride in mental growth incited in any comparable fashion. One of the outstanding leaders of this century attributed his success to a mother who encouraged him in his mental development and who gave her most valuable rewards for the achievements of mental growth in his religious life.

Jesus' mental growth, however, included both knowledge and wisdom. He became not only smarter but wiser. Those who did mental battle with him discovered that he had a trained mind, well supplied with the ammunition of knowledge, and that he was also mentally agile and clever. And those who sought desperately help and advice for themselves found in him a depth of understanding and an ability to resolve the difficulties of living which enabled him to speak to their need "as no man ever spoke" (John 7:46). Wisdom comes from a way of looking at life. It requires the long view, the high view, and the broad view. Foolishness and shortsightedness are often bedfellows. Yet "What is there in it for me now?" has become the popular stimulus for many life-determining mental reactions.

Jesus had a dedicated mind. Early in life he found a supreme attachment for it in God. Every worthy cause to which he gave intellectual approval had to qualify through co-ordination with this highest commitment. He believed that love for God was an intellectual as well as an emotional experience and, therefore, commanded his followers to love God with all their minds. It would be a most rewarding study to trace the influences for good which came into the life of Jesus and through him to others' lives because of this dedication of his mind. It gave unity to his life and its activities. It supplied a mental stimulus to be ever learning. It kept his thought on a high level. It sustained his love of good life and his respect for his fellow man. It rewarded him for his service to others. It solved the riddle of life's undeserved crosses. It immunized him from frustration and cynicism. It strengthened him to withstand the pressures of wrong thinking and to unmask the philosophies of life which destroy. About every good thing one can say of the life which Jesus lived had its source in the dedication of his mind to know and to serve God. And about every good thing man now strives for and finds so illusive Jesus achieved through his mental commitment to the truth in God.

So the Christian mind is not an indeterminate phrase subject only to argument and speculation. Enough is known of it in the experience of Jesus to keep modern man busy with its provisions and to justify his commitment to it by the decided improvement which has never failed to accompany a conscious dedication of the mind to the highest.

Like Alexander, seeking the conquest of the world through giving the world a Greek mind, so for the Christianization of life all the educational forces will have to unite upon the task of "[putting] the mind of one man into many a life." It must become a conscious purpose and the object of an aggressive campaign of Christian education. No compromise or lower standard can be tolerated if the Christian imprint is to give life its character.

How to implant this mental point of view against so much active opposition and cultivate it amid so many adverse circumstances also find workable suggestions through Jesus' experience.

The story of Jesus provides a history of education for a Christian mind. When we look at the Jesus of history instead of the Jesus of theology, a workable plan for giving to the young a Christian mind clearly emerges. Through Christ we see how to relate all the contacts of life to that goal. He demonstrated how every experience in life can be enlisted in the service of the best.

First of all, there was his knowledge of the divine purpose. Jesus believed he came from God. So must all of us believe that. God had a plan for Jesus' life and for every other life. It is inconceivable to think of God as neutral or disinterested in the development of his creation. God is on the side of the Christian imprint for every life. This divine relationship to what we are and what we may become was very real to the parents and friends of Jesus and to Jesus himself. The consciousness of this relationship was a deciding factor in the choices he made. It was responsible for victory when the logic of events predicted defeat. When it drops out of man's thinking, as it largely has today, life takes on the prevailing patterns of convenience rather than the pattern of Christ.

Jesus' parents also were conscious of a divine purpose in his his life and of their obligation to further it. They thought of their child as a gift from God with a place to fill in his plan and of their privilege to further that plan and to help their child to see it. Just as Augustine said he "drank in Christ with his mother's milk," so the imprint on an infant's life begins to take form from the thoughts which the parents have regarding his origin and destiny and their transmission to the child through their attitude and example.

The school he attended contributed to his knowledge by teaching the morality of God and documenting it by the lessons of history. The responsibility of the school to implant the religious knowledge of life was unquestioned in Hebrew society. Their teachers were trained to put this religious content into the education of the young. According to an interpretation of traditional American education by a Kansas Supreme Court, "The public still has a right to demand of the teacher that the pupil shall come out with a more acute sense of right and wrong, higher ideals of life, a higher conception of duty as a citizen, and a more laudable ambition in life than when he entered." But how can this be done unless the pupil is furnished with a perspective of life which includes the story of mankind in relation to God?

The elders likewise advanced this knowledge by giving attention to the serious questions of the young. Jesus' treatment in the Temple, when the learned doctors of the law took time to answer the simple but searching questions of the boy whose religious curiosity was recognized as a natural part of his growing life, should give modern parents, who brush off such questions, and the "learned" teachers of the present, who treat them with humor or cynicism, cause to think of their response to the young in the light of future judgment.

The Church had a part in developing the Christian mind of

Jesus. Not always sympathetic and understanding, it was, however, the open sesame through worship and fellowship for many of Jesus' spiritual insights and for the testing of those insights through service to others.

Jesus' life in its final fruition was the product of all it had touched. His friends, his experiences, even his enemies, brought out the lines of the Christian life which he himself had come consciously to desire and God had encouraged in personal experiences which clarified and strengthened both the Christian objective for his life and his purpose to achieve and maintain it.

No doubt many questions could be raised concerning the feasibility of these methods for developing and maintaining the Christian mind within the present environment. Times change, we are told. But the standard by which to judge these methods is the result which would be achieved in the human mind if they were intelligently and sincerely followed in the education of the young. If parents took Mary and Joseph's attitude, if schools recognized their responsibility for religious education, if elders took seriously the religious questions of the young, if churches tried to make their services experiences of spiritual growth and a proving ground through directed activity for the truth of their insight, if the child was encouraged to think of himself as God's person and to expect God's guidance revealed to him in practical ways, under such a program of education no one could deny that great improvement in the quality of life would follow.

THE CHRISTIAN DOCTRINE OF THE SPIRIT

Christian education, however, holds that maintaining the Christian imprint upon life is in the final analysis a spiritual achievement. Improved environment, mental growth, and co-operating people make a most valuable contribution to the experience of Christian living; but it survives and renews itself by the quality of its spiritual content. Favorable circumstances will not preserve the Christian imprint if it crumbles from within. Something must give the Christian life a temper, that is, a consistency, a hardness, and a toughness, which enables it to retain its distinctiveness and identity in spite of the pressures and the abrasive forces which would eradicate it.

The present age has experienced its most costly failures at this point. Often the advances made in the conditions of living through the knowledge of better living and by the united efforts of participating groups are offset or destroyed altogether because of spiritual immaturity and malnutrition. We show growth in every way except growth toward God. The spiritual thinness of life cannot provide the strength to live up to life's physical, intellectual, and social capabilities. Persons ample in body but meager in soul do not create the Christian imprint for themselves, nor do they leave its mark on society.

Jesus' growth included the spirit. He grew in favor with God. (Luke 2:52.) He became more rather than less at home in the divine presence as he moved from childhood to manhood—an order of spiritual movement which modern life has largely reversed. What contributed to his deepening spiritual experience is important knowledge for an age which has largely lost its childhood awareness of God.

In providing a Christian doctrine of the spirit from which the Christian imprint takes form and by which it maintains its identity, it is well to remember that even with such a responsive person as Jesus it was held in mind as a conscious part of his education. What he learned of God and the spirit was not left to chance as so often such knowledge is today. It followed a pattern which touched and molded his life in at least five determinative places.

First, a spiritual content and meaning were given to his origin. Mary and Joseph believed that Jesus was sent to them from God and that they were under the divine direction and obligation in their care of him. How his parents thought of his coming formed the first impressions he had of his origin. Thus Jesus from the beginning sensed that in some personal way he came from God and went to God. This consciousness explains the high and consistent spiritual achievement of his life. Physical origins are a fact about human life, but not its explanation. Sex education, concerned with physical life and social adjustment, deals with production and not origin. And unless education roots life in God it cannot produce either the flower or fruitage of Christian living. From Jesus we learn the important lesson that the child's conception of his origin determines the man's fulfillment of his destiny.

Jesus was aided also in producing and preserving the Christian imprint by a Christian concept of his world supported by the processes of reasoning. To him it was a spiritual creation. His entire life indicated his early acquaintance with the twenty-fourth psalm, which, like much of the scriptures learned by Hebrew youth, he was taught to repeat before he could fully comprehend its meaning. But from it he got a point of view which made him think of the world in which he lived, not as a commodity, but as a trust. It was his Father's world.

> The earth is the Lord's and the fulness thereof,
> the world and those who dwell therein.

The frame of reference in which he lived his life was within the creating and redeeming orbit of God's plan and power. It is easier in the spiritual climate of the present to think of God's plan for a life than it is to think of God's plan for the world. Both, however, have been largely ignored or forgotten. Yet the spiritual meaning of the world for us is essential for the spiritual meaning of our lives; and until we re-establish God as the architect and man as the builder in popular thinking, the power to redeem the world will elude even the cleverest and most courageous generation.

Jesus learned and used the language of the spirit. Not only did he possess a vocabulary of spiritual words, but he knew their spiritual meaning. Words are symbols which express ideas and concepts. They can be used, however, without transmitting the meaning of the ideas they stand for. This has happened to the spiritual vocabulary of the present generation. Either spiritual and ecclesiastical terms have become a dead language which the typical person does not use at all, or the terms used have been robbed of their spiritual or supernatural connotations. For instance, it makes a difference whether in speaking of God we mean a convenient term for the sum of human values or the Father of our Lord and Saviour Jesus Christ. The current call for a return to faith is significant only when we know what is meant by it. Is it a humanistic device only, meaning trust and confidence in man's own power and in one another? Or is it the faith which Jesus had in God, who to him was creator, sustainer, guide, and redeemer? This generation is little advanced in spiritual knowledge beyond the people of Ephesus, who when Paul inquired concerning their acquaintance with the Holy Spirit, admitted that they did not know what he was talking about. Spiritual knowledge cannot be communicated unless there is a common acquaintance with its vocabulary and a common understanding of the meaning of the words used.

Jesus developed a working understanding of spiritual authority. The voice of God was the voice of authority. What did he mean by that? To him the voice of authority was not personal desire, nor was it the word of the majority, both of which are current standards for human action. It was the word of scripture; it was the experience of men and nations in applying that word to life. It was an inner voice, often drowned out by the din of modern living, which could always be validated by the good its directives would accomplish. To Jesus this authority was final and obligatory, the first and basic requirement for God's life and power in man's life and world. It was the one thing without which no permanent improvement could come. The

112

discipline of authority, lost in the first part of the twentieth century, emerges as a requirement for salvation in the second half of this century.

Jesus had a clear conception of the spiritual function of his life. To the question "What is life?" he had a satisfying answer which did not leave him either satiated, frustrated, or despairing. The spiritual function which his life was to perform in the plan of God gave it meaning, importance, and quality. In other words, Jesus was conscious of the higher functions of life and of its eternal significance. The secondary functions, physical, material, and temporal, were guided and determined by a divine purpose. Often this purpose is called vocation. It means simply doing the will of God, living up to the highest as revealed in Christ, wherever you are and whatever you are called on to do.

Meaning is the one thing lacking in so many today who possess all the other qualifications for satisfying and effective living. Motivation which does not rise above self-interest is never sufficient to lift life to a plane of Christian living. Nevertheless the educational influences preparing the young today pitch life on the physical, material, and temporal levels when they ignore the fact of a spiritual function above the purely self-created plans for life investment.

The spiritual content of Jesus' life was, of course, the genius of his well-rounded maturity. It is the point at which modern education has done its poorest job; and the home, church, and community, as well as the school, must share the blame.

THE CHRISTIAN DOCTRINE OF SOCIETY

Even Jesus, the divine Son of God, separate, unique, and above the common level of man, could not live his life in a vacuum of nonsocial activity, nor dwell constantly in the ivory tower of some mount of Transfiguration. "None of us lives to himself." (Rom. 14: bye What he was and what he did depended

* Wand, *op. cit.*

upon his relation to others. This fact is true of all life, and for the good life the Christian doctrine of society is essential.

The recognition of the need for the right kind of human relations is widely acknowledged. Certainly in every phase of life it is being talked about. No "education for responsible living" can ignore it, for as Wallace B. Donham pointed out in a book by that title, "the most important aspect of human knowledge and experience is human relations."

The distressing expression of human relations on all levels is, however, an indication that the education of the individual for life with others has not been effective. It needs to be restudied in the light of past experience and present necessities. Many studies of this nature which have been conducted have failed largely in changing human relations for the better because they have dealt too much with superficial causes and the current manifestation of symptoms rather than the sources out of which the current maladjustments of people to one another have sprung.

Youth and their delinquencies, while affording the occasion for such investigations, are not the place to begin the search for causes and for cures. Experience past and present leads to the older generation as the ground for discovering what can be done to improve the human relations of the rising generation. Alfred North Whitehead, commenting in conversation on the breakdown of society, held parents responsible. He said:

For parents having lost their own belief go on insisting on the dead formulae of conduct in order to keep their children "good" when they no longer believed these formulae themselves. Then children eventually found it out and between the ages of 18 and 24, when one is experiencing for the first time vital necessities, emotional and physical, were left in total ignorance of the social consequences of certain types of conduct.[4]

4 *The Dialogues of Alfred North Whitehead*, ed. Lucien Price (Little, Brown & Co.).

Whitehead's observation is simply the rediscovery of the truth of this matter which is inherent in the Christian doctrine of society. As far back as David's time parental derelictions were seen as the cause of the social maladjustments of the young. This was the explanation for Adonijah's tragic experience with life. "His father [Haggith] had never at any time displeased him by asking, 'Why have you done thus and so?'" (I Kings 1:6). So when he was surrounded by David's men, he rushed "and caught hold of the horns of the altar"; but then it was too late for religion to save him from the consequences of his bad education.

Society is failing to solve its basic problem, which is the art of living together in a world of differences, because its pattern is defective; and its adult demonstrators, themselves the victims of a bungled upbringing, have not been willing to improve it. Self-interest has been the most prominent appeal made for better human relations, and it is not a sufficient motive for real brotherhood. Yet that is still the chief incitement for personal effort in getting along with others and for the political arrangements of profitable coexistence. Brotherhood with only the binder of self-interest lacks the cohesiveness to hold a good society together under the pressure of greedy forces both from within man's own nature and from the highly organized attack of the evil forces which surround his life.

The needed element is a Christian doctrine of society, a belief about oneself and others which binds individuals, separately and together, to the best. It was the consciousness of this doctrine which gave Jesus power to help and to influence people. He grew in this knowledge and its uses. He made it an objective of his life and a measure of its success. In his parents and their friends, such as Elizabeth and Zachariah, Simeon and Anna, he first beheld its glimmerings. In association with them his footsteps were started in the path which brought him increasing favor with man. (Luke 2:52.) From their limited knowledge he found the keys which opened the doors to the highest knowledge of human and divine interrelatedness. And without these factors all man's modern clever and novel techniques for producing and guaranteeing good human relations will fail.

The Christian imprint on society can be maintained only by what strengthens and protects it from within. It is what a person has come to believe about himself and others which determines the outcome. Wrong beliefs nurtured in the twentieth century have shown up in an ugly, gross, and twisted world society which the common man knows must be changed. But changed to what and by what methods are still unknown to many who have grown up in the Christian tradition without having got much of that tradition on the inside of them.

How Jesus grew in these relations must become the model of living and the method of education if a Christian imprint is to be stamped on society. His doctrine of human relations must be understood and applied by all who would attain his gifts in dealing with people and who would build a society which enables people to live together in Christian fellowship.

The Christian doctrine of society, as Jesus demonstrated it, stands out in five particulars when contrasted to the current ideas about human relations.

The first concerns the source of good human relations. While the present generation is absorbed in creating the mechanical, economic, and social devices which facilitate and safeguard their corporate existence, the Christian sees in the life of Jesus these relations as the expression of an organic brotherhood which has its source in a divine fatherhood. In the Christian doctrine of society brotherhood without fatherhood is an anomaly. It lacks life and the power to survive. It may be perfect organization, but it has no cohesiveness sufficient to hold it together under the pressure of individual self-interest. A Christian society gets its creative and sustaining power from God and not man.

In contrast to the self-centered attitude of the present generation, which lives as if the world should revolve around it, Jesus found the center of life in God and organized all life's activities around him. It was the Father's will and not the individual's desire which was to determine how a person should live with himself and with others. Jesus showed the way to avoid the anarchy in human relations which plagues this century by relating all men to a common center higher and outside themselves. Changing the center of human activities from the individual to his Creator and from a self-ordained leadership such as totalitarianism has produced to a divine center around which a universal brotherhood, diverse in its component parts, can revolve is a task for education. Its first step is to relate the child to God and to others in ways which make the child an adjunct to them rather than to make them the instruments for the child's self-centered satisfactions. It must require the disciplines of living together while learning the arts of living. Its concern for the discovery of new techniques in human relations must be anchored in both religious knowledge and human experience. It must acquaint the individual with the truths of good human relations which, while yielding to adjustment, can never be compromised if they are to produce the fruits of Christian brotherhood.

Much of this type of education has been dropped in an indulgent era which has encouraged individuals in clinging to wrong ideas about themselves and discounted the disciplines which are required for helpful human relations.

Jesus looked at society with a new sense of the basic value of each of its members. They were all, regardless of class or heritage or political and geographical grouping, of equal and of highest value in the sight of God. This was a new and strange theory of man and society in Jesus' time; and while theoretically accepted by Christians today, in its practical application it still appears new and strange. People admit this universal brotherhood but do not live by its truths nor act on its precepts.

It is the Christian doctrine of man which lifted him from the category of a commodity. Jesus brought up to the level of human realization the fact that a man is of more value than a sheep and, therefore, is not for sale, nor can he be used as a mere pawn on the chessboard of political and social manipulation. The most potent reminder of the equal and high value of all men in the sight of God, regardless of their present state or anti-social activity, is the fact that Jesus died for everyone. It is, alas, the most impelling motive for service on behalf of others. This is a concept of man, religious and Christian, for which education has never found an effective substitute. It is the most beneficial antidote to self-centeredness available to a society suffering from too much vitamin "I." Its significance and application to life must find their way back into man's attitude toward others.

The Christian doctrine of society supplies man with a different and much-needed standard of personal and corporate action. The current attitude of "What is there in it for me?" has greatly retarded man's corporate efforts to withstand evil and to advance the good. Twentieth-century philosophies of life have based their appeal on taking what another has for oneself rather than on defending the right and creating the good for the benefit of all. Little by little modern man has been losing his life by trying to save it for himself alone until a generation has been educated to reject the altruistic appeal of doing good for the sake of the good.

Jesus brought to his age a new standard for human activities inherent in man's nature, but undeveloped and unawakened both then and now. It replaced the self-centered attitude of "Why should I?" with the self-challenging question "What can I do?" The presence of the bad was a call to do good. It changed the motive of action from taking what one can for oneself to making better everything associated with life. And a world which is actually seeking a Christian brotherhood, whether it is conscious of what it seeks or not, must be made acquainted with the standards of that brotherhood and must be trained in the activities and attitudes which will etch its lines more deeply upon life. The Christian imprint to avoid social distortions must be constantly checked by the Christian standard.

Jesus brought to the Christian content of good human relations a new and enduring objective. Where his contemporaries had a personal or a political objective for what they did with and for others, Jesus made a new order of life his goal. He saw the higher fellowship resulting from a new spirit in life which he called the kingdom of God. The phrase was misunderstood by his hearers, and it has a ring of unreality for many today. We have been trained to think in terms of doing rather than being, of actions rather than attitudes, and of forms of association rather than the quality of society's constituent parts. So by wrong education regarding the social spirit our generation suffers from organized evil just as did the generation of Jesus.

A Christian content and meaning must be given to the conception of the society we seek to produce before we can make our hopes and achievements for our life together coincide. The good society must be taught as a sacrament—"an outward and visible sign of an inward and spiritual grace." The projection of the kingdom of God which has already come within. "The life of Jesus . . . manifested in our mortal flesh." (II Cor. 4:11.)

So long as the by-products of a Christian society, such as peace, prosperity, literacy, leisure, and comfort, are held up as final objectives, the source and guarantee of these by-products will continue to elude mankind; and the by-products themselves are likely to be little more than counterfeits. Education in its varied ways of developing the individual must set his sights on a Christian society, founded on Christ, ordained of God, known as the kingdom of heaven, and coming first within his own life.

The consciousness of what one does, why one does it, and what he intends to accomplish by it is basic to the development and preservation of free men and a Christian society. Without

119

this the outward Christian form can be easily altered. Failing to have it, the individual loses his way in this modern network of highways for living. His inspiration and his courage ebb. His incentive no longer matches the struggle. At first he compromises, and finally he submits.

All of this we have seen happen to a generation educated in a free and "Christian" world—educated, it was supposed, to perpetuate the forms of a free and Christian society without having a knowledge of what that life consists nor the reasons for creating and nurturing it.

And all of this calls for replacement by Christian ideas for society if a Christian world fellowship rather than the extension of social services becomes the objective of free people. "This," according to Sir Richard Livingstone, "is a task of education in the widest sense and needs first an educational system which will make it possible and next, within that system, an education which will achieve it." [5]

[5] *Op. cit.* Used by permission of Cambridge University Press.

CHAPTER V

THE FINISHED WORK

*As therefore you received Christ Jesus the Lord, so live in him,
rooted and built up in him, . . . seeing that you have put
off the old nature with its practices and have put on the new nature,
which is being renewed in knowledge after the image of its
creator, . . . until we all attain . . . to mature manhood,
to the measure of the stature of the fullness of Christ.*
                                                    —COL. 2:6-7; 3:9-10; EPH. 4:13

WE COME NOW TO THE FINAL QUESTIONS RELATING TO THE
development of the Christian imprint. They have to do with its
distinctive nature and with the steps required to make it last.
It is possible to come to the end of an earnest endeavor and discover that what was supposed to be the outcome is not what is
finally produced. A bit of "iron-curtain" humor relates a story
of a factory worker who supposed that he and his associates
were producing the parts for baby carriages. Needing one and
finding no provision for it in the planned economy which controlled his income and expenditures, he began to filch the parts
which were being made in the departments of the factory.
Finally, however, when he had accumulated them all and fitted
them together, what he had did not even resemble a baby carriage. It turned out to be a machine gun.

In any process which calls for a number of contributing factors constant checking is required to insure the intended outcome. One defective part can spoil the final product. Improper

co-ordination of the various steps in the process can have the same effect. Stopping the operation before all the necessary procedures have been completed renders ineffective all that has been previously well done. Workmen inattentive to the blueprints will mutilate the best materials. So to be certain that the finished work meets the original expectations, the end result must be kept constantly in sight and the contributing operations for its consummation meticulously performed.

The finished work of Christian education is subject to all these requirements. If it is to succeed in its task, it must have at all times a clear conception of its objective. All its contributing participants—parents in the home, teachers in the schools, citizens in the community—must be skilled in performing their part. Each must be fitted together in correct sequence and in proper proportions. No step can be omitted, and the work must carry through to the end. Fidelity in craftsmanship, as well as teamwork in production, must be united if the goal for Christian education is to be attained.

THE GOAL OF CHRISTIAN EDUCATION

What then is the finished work of all Christian education? What is the goal which each factor influencing the outcome must keep clearly in mind? Paul, the father of Christian education and a qualified expert in its application to life, said that it was a full-grown man, mature in Christ. (Eph. 4:13.) Always the goal of Christian education is a special person, an individual with personality distinctions which set him apart and easily identify him. No expertness of skill and no combination of resources can substitute for a person-centered concern in education in either the home or the school if the producing of a special person is the outcome sought. Many contributing factors are necessary for this completed process, but they cannot attain the goal in and of themselves. Nor can they make their full contribution unless they are properly co-ordinated in the work. Always there is the danger that an overconcern for the means to attain the goal will reduce the effort to achieve the end for which the means are provided. An overconfidence in some phase of the total process of Christian education is a constant deterrent to the development of the mature man whose life reflects the fullness of Christ. Doctrinal provisions, organizational achievements, and statistical goals often tempt the Christian educator to make them rather than the person they affect the terminal of their effort. While the provision of theological doctrine and a philosophy for Christian education provide a necessary background for the work of Christian education, by themselves doctrine and philosophy do not create the life they describe. "The demons believed." They could pass an examination on doctrine. But they still remain demons. The implementation of organization, methods, and equipment is an important help too often neglected in the process of developing a person to mature Christian manhood. Yet the most complete provision of mechanical and physical facilities will turn out only character blanks unless purposeful hands use them as tools. The urgency for mass production, a task which Christian education needs to work on around the world, is essential for the widest intellectual, social, and evangelical Christian outreach. But if the activities of mass efforts are a mere spinning of the wheels of the educational machinery the assembly line will simply return the human materials passing over it somewhat damaged or unchanged. The moral responsibilities for Christian education, which should be a compulsion to activity when undertaken solely as a duty, also produce disappointing results. "I tried to do my duty" is the wail of many a distracted parent who sees his child responding to the wrong stimuli in life. Nevertheless these moral responsibilities, which need a wide revival in home, school, and community, are touched with power only when they carry a person beyond the line of duty in a labor of love for others. The extras of love, service, prayer, knowledge, and example quicken duty with life-giving

123

powers in producing this special person. Christian education must also pay attention to the general welfare if it is to create the conditions within which the Christian imprint emerges most prominently and has an environment conducive to its preservation. Yet we have seen how an absorbing interest in general conditions, when detached from the proper molding of individuals who live in the improved environment, has failed either to deepen or to retain the Christian imprint upon social cultures and their institutions. Socially and economically a world can get better while morally and spiritually it grows worse. All of these concerns of Christian education are essential as steps toward the final goal. Drop out any one of them, and the resultant persons produced will be something less than the expectations. On the other hand, overemphasis of one at the expense of the other produces a distorted Christian personality. When they are looked on as ends in themselves, the most unstinted labor in their behalf will fail to mark a single life with the image of Christ. Directed, however, toward the maturing person, to the full stature of Christian character and personality, they never fail to succeed.

Making the goal of Christian education person centered has behind it also the authority and example of the Master Teacher. His method was to hand-pick and hand-tool individuals for the Christian life. His teachings, which form the basis for Christian doctrine, and his miracles, which dramatically symbolized his power, often overshadow in our thought the real sources out of which his way of life grew and multiplied. These sources were his personal contacts and endeavors. He called to himself individuals. Before they saw him, he had seen them. Not only did he pick and train his disciples in this personal way, but likewise in the crowds he was alert to contacts with the persons who composed them. The crowd was never just a sea of faces to him. No doubt his attitude toward people sprang from an emulation of his Father's personal interest in his creation. His example was the best proof he could offer that our heavenly Father knows us all by name. No person was ever lost in the crowd to Jesus. Sometimes people lost him in the crowd as so often happens today because of the impersonal ways of bigness. They forgot that regardless of circumstances each one was a special concern to God. But when men remembered, no matter how great the press, they could always get Jesus' eye. Zacchaeus, the ill woman, and blind Bartimaeus all secured the special attention of Jesus in spite of the pressing demands of the milling throngs. Jesus recognized the importance of making those whom he would change feel his personal concern for them.

Now this sense of personal interest is the most powerful force in Christian human relations. Making a person feel that he counts establishes the atmosphere most conducive to changing one life through the influence of another. Yet it has always been a major problem in education. Endless arguments go on about the merits of the various methods for keeping the personal relation between teacher and pupil, parent and child, adult and youth, the leader and the rank and file. Often the debate swings to numbers and centers in the arguments for and against the mass approach or the individual approach. The big school or the little one, the large church or the small one, the city or the village, mass evangelism or personal evangelism, business' inaccessible policy maker or the executive with an open door, all are debated in relation to whether or not they help or hinder the goal of all human relations, which is an improved life. But the power to touch and to change a person is not so much a physical matter as it is a psychical one. Some persons with an audience of one could never make it, while Jesus in the throngs always created an atmosphere of personal interest. It is a quality of the molder, whoever he may be, rather than a condition under which he does his work. It results from a conscious objective on the part of those who would influence others as well as from an expectant relation in the approach of those who are influenced. Bigness and numbers are no hindrance to this personal relationship of molder and the molded provided the necessities for maintaining it in mass movements and large groups are recognized and provided for.

Christian education weakens its power when it succumbs to the allurements of impersonalism in its human relations. Each child in the family, each pupil in the class, each contact in the community, calls for an evident personal interest and a studied individual treatment if the imprint of Christ is to be etched by it. No one law covers all, and no one method can be counted on to get results in every case. Some Christian workers try to produce Christian persons like the billboard artist who puts the same facial features on everybody he paints. Christian personality yields to a mold but each after his own kind and according to his own nature. This distinction is seen in the differences evident in children in the same home with the same heredity, environment, and opportunity. Each calls for special handling in the development of his finest traits of character and in the control of the less attractive aspects of his personality.

How well Jesus knew this, and how expertly he dealt with each individual according to the nature of his need and personality. His way with Peter differed from his way with John. Martha needed a different treatment from Mary. Watch him exercising this principle in his daily ministries. To one he says, "Your sins are forgiven," and to another, "Rise and walk." To one rich man he says, "Make haste . . . ; for I must stay at your house today," and to another, "Sell all that you have." At times he says, "Pray"; and at other times he says, "Work." Under one set of conditions he bids his special pupils to "Let the children come to me," and in another he directs them to give the crowd something to eat. Jesus fitted his relations to the need and the nature of those he would win and change.

To be sure, this personal approach and individual treatment seemed slow. It required long hours of tedious work. And it was constantly under question by Jesus' impatient associates who wanted the Kingdom to come right away. It was, indeed, as a grain of mustard seed. But Jesus saw in this one-by-one method what those closest to him and what so many today, conditioned to think of success only in terms of bigness, had overlooked. He saw its potentialities. He sensed its creativeness. He knew its power to set in motion a chain reaction. His way was like leaven. It kept multiplying. Once started it could not be stopped. Surely the evidences of its soundness were demonstrated by the new life and its resultant civilization which emerged in the first centuries. That era became dated by it. And what, may be asked, is the hope of survival for the Christian imprint upon life today, especially in those sections of the world where the philosophy of life is changing and the organization of Christian activity disintegrates? At home, where so much of the tried and tested truths about life is forgotten, and behind the iron curtains, where so many of the Christian ways are prohibited, what is the hope of a survival of the changing work of Christ upon the lives of men? Is it not the touch of a loving and a molding hand upon the deep springs of another's life, the marks upon one's nature and character which environmental conditions may darken for a time but never eradicate? Modern conditions are driving us to a new realization that the survival of a pattern of life is assured, not by the clamping down of external requirements, but by the irresistible emerging of deep impressions upon man's imperishable nature. That is both the Christian hope and the Christian's task.

THE MARKS OF THE CHRISTIAN IMPRINT

Knowing how to put a lasting imprint upon the lives of others and to insure its survival and duplication among the generations which will follow, do we with sufficient clarity and definiteness know what the distinctive marks of that Christian imprint actually are? Can it be said that parents in any large numbers have a clear conception of what they are working toward in the maturing of their children? Is not this uncertainty the real point at issue in the babel of confused debate with regard to religious teaching in the public schools? Is not the good citizen often hard put to express exactly what he is working toward through his personal example and welfare activities? When asked, "What do you expect to accomplish, and what specific changes shall follow in community life?" he realizes that in his enthusiasm for the process he has failed to find out its objective.

The indefiniteness which has surrounded the marks of the Christian pattern for life has deterred its imprint and marred its quality. It has opened the way for the caricature prodigals of the Christian life by the fanatics, and it has discouraged genuine effort to produce that imprint on the part of those who by inclination and training could best reproduce it. One senses this indistinctness in the hesitancy with which so many church members answer the question "Are you a Christian?" They evade the answer more often because they are not sure of the requirements than because they are conscious that they have not met them. Like the Corinthians on whom Paul worked to imprint the image of Christ, modern man is too often untrained to "recognize that Jesus Christ is in you." (II Cor. 13:5.)[1] In dealing with all age groups the plea for definiteness in describing the nature and marks of the Christian life is insistent. They ask simply for a plain answer. They want to see the outline of the Christian features. They ask for an acquaintance with its character manifestations. Delicate shadings and the theoretical debates of the experts can and should await this basic instruction. The artist begins a portrait with a charcoal sketch. He outlines the subject. He adjusts the parts in their proper proportion. Then he mixes his paints for color and shading and fills in the form. The form may be thought of as fact. That is how the subject is. The painting is interpretation. It is the artist's way of making it live. Now in producing the Christian imprint we need to follow the artist's order, which in much of the current Protestant approach to

Christian living we have reversed. We must begin with the charcoal sketch, as it were. We must start with the common facts of form. We must get a pattern of the Christian life in its proper proportions before we go into the more technical and often debatable questions of shades of meaning and niceties of distinctions and the values of individual interpretation. The one must follow the other if we attain the image which expresses the fullness of Christ. But the basic lines must come first; and in so much of the Protestant approach they are either assumed or overlooked with the result that the rank and file who are trying to put the image of Christ upon life either do poor work or give up altogether.

Paul, who pioneered in all this field of Christian education and who earned the titles of theologian, teacher, and evangelist, addressed himself to both phases in the production of the Christian image—its "charcoal drawing," or its basic form; and the final "oil painting" with its interpretative colorings, lines, and shadings.

He began with the fundamentals, and he made them distinguishable by directing attention to the marks of the Christian image which he bore in his own body. (Gal. 6:17.) People recognized the outline of the Christian pattern because Paul made them see it in him. From there he proceeded to enrich and to interpret it in his theology, discussing the optional and the debatable and lifting out the overtones for the appreciation of those who had advanced that far in their appreciation and skill.

To restore a definiteness to the Christian imprint so that it can be recognized by those who seek it and would reproduce it is basic to its mature expression in the finished work of a Christian life.

The image of Christ in you, what should it reveal? The finished work, how can it be distinguished? When you start out to produce it, what do you see as the form it should take? Paul in his instruction dealt with these questions. In what might be called

his lessons on the Christian imprint, he lifted up four characteristics of the mature Christian which give him form and show
forth his distinguishing marks. They all involve a relationship
to Christ, the master Christian, and are basic for the development
of Christ's life in man.

CHARACTERISTICS OF CHRISTIAN MATURITY

First, Paul said the finished work should reveal a man in Christ,
and we must learn in practical terms what Paul meant by this
phrase if we are to experience this relationship ourselves and
help others to attain it. So often the finer meanings of religion
elude us because of our unfamiliarity with the language used.
Religious phraseology is often difficult to understand because
it is not related to man's common experiences and daily conduct.
For this reason Paul's language sometimes takes on an unreality
for its current readers which certainly was not present when
it was first expressed. This reaction to Paul's instruction sometimes occurs because we think of him as a theologian rather than
as a man of practical affairs. Paul spoke to the inexperienced and
the unlettered. They understood the language which this modern
age has trouble with. It was a potent medium for bringing new
life to them. And for those now engaged in producing the Christian imprint upon life the recapture of the life-transforming
meaning in Paul's teaching gives tremendous power.

The Christian imprint according to Paul is an incarnation. It
is a spiritual experience in which God permeates every phase
of a person's being. When it happens, something of God is evident in every expression of one's life and work. Paul used many
phrases to express this relationship of man and God. Some of
them this generation has mistaken for boasting and in disavowing
them has lost the spiritual experience which they expressed. It
helps in attaining and maintaining a relationship to become
openly committed to it. Public, as well as private, commitment
to the best is a psychological necessity in the spiritual life of man.

Paul saw this new life emerging when Christ was absorbed in man's nature. It was a relationship in which Christ was not taken on as a possession but in which man was possessed by Christ. When we say that a person is all wrapped up in something so that he eats it and sleeps it, we approximate Paul's meaning in his expression that Christ was all and in all. The modern observation that we think alike matches Paul's exhortation to "let this mind be in you, which was also in Christ Jesus" (Phil. 2:5 K.J.V.). Sometimes we say of a person he is his father all over again; and thinking in spiritual terms, we can see through it what Paul meant when he said Christ dwelled in him. By being in Christ, Paul thought of a spiritual identification, a meeting of minds, a pooling of actions, and a harmony of life. It is an at-one-ment with Christ. Thought of in a terminology which describes in current terms human reactions, the phrase "a man in Christ" no longer appears hazy, nor does it sound archaic. It can be grasped by the youngest and its deeper meanings become comprehensible to the most sophisticated. Paul described a very practical experience as a first characteristic of the Christian imprint.

Furthermore, this relationship, when established, brought with it certain identifying powers which indicated its presence and its genuineness. It empowers a person for sustained action on the highest levels of life. For, as Paul wrote to the Christians in Rome, only those who are in Christ are capable of rising to the full height of the moral law. Loving one's enemies, returning good for evil, putting the best interpretation on the actions of others, the gentle tongue, the broad understanding, bigness in the presence of littleness, are all the lines of character which appear when Christ is in a person and permeates his entire being. Now and again these distinctive Christian characteristics appear in persons who do not acknowledge this total acceptance of Christ in life. But like the century plant their bloom of beauty

[1] Wand, *op. cit.*

and goodness is infrequent. With one whose life is absorbed in Christ these and a host of other distinctly Christian reactions become perennial.

In the scheme of influences through which God works, the effort to make this relationship to Christ attractive and practical is the medium by which it takes hold and reproduces itself. It is not so much a transmission, as in the case of factual knowledge or theological doctrine, as it is an awakening. Something happens within in response to the outward stimuli of teaching and example by which a person sees himself and Christ in an identity of spirit and, desiring it with a consuming passion, realizes that the way is plain and clear for him to have it.

Paul's second distinctive feature of the Christian portrait is Christlikeness. The spirit of a man who is truly one with Christ expresses itself in his conduct. A man in Christ will be a man like Christ. To the first Christians this relationship was axiomatic. Expressing Christ's spirit in their daily life was a mark of discipleship. At times it made them different from others, and at times they practiced Christ's way of living to their own immediate disadvantage. They recognized the denials of popular ways of living which it demanded and accepted a discipline of conduct as a medium for the attainment of an unhampered spiritual relationship with Christ. Their actions, they knew, could impede the growth of the spirit.

These first Christians were marked men and women. But their marks were badges of quality and not expressions of peculiarities. This characteristic became the strongest witness for the reality and validity of the Christian faith. Their sole defense and only weapon was a life of integrity (II Cor. 6 Phillips). The one unanswerable argument for Christianity in the early centuries was "See how the Christians live!" Their life was their message.

The emphasis upon conduct as a distinctive mark of a Christian is still to be seen in the lives of the members of the so-called young churches, that is, the churches on the mission fields. When the Chinese say of a person, "He is a Christian," much more is meant by it than our Western use of the term denotes. They are not simply identifying a person's religious faith by using a label, which is the common usage of it in the Western world. They mean that in all phases of the person's life and conduct he can be trusted, for he is Christlike. Christ is that person's example and determines what his attitude should be. (Phil. 2:5.)

For the Western world the term "he is a Christian" has lost much of its distinctiveness. It is used more often to indicate a religious category than it is to describe a way of life. The hesitancy on the part of so many church members to confess publicly that they are Christians is indicative of the confused meaning of the term in their thinking. Paul's conception of it certainly went beyond a cataloguing of one's religious faith or a legalistic relationship to that faith. It meant a way of life which was expressed in conduct, an imprint which could be seen in one's actions. It stood as an outward and visible sign of an inward and spiritual experience.

Christian ethics and morality have had a hard time keeping alive in the twentieth century. The demands of a continued political and economic crisis have nearly submerged a consideration of Christian principles as a basis for human judgment and conduct. Christian morality and ethics have been both compromised and camouflaged until they are hardly distinguishable. The most graphic way to see what has happened to the Christian conduct of life is to put the Ten Commandments and the Sermon on the Mount and the thirteenth chapter of First Corinthians beside a day's activities of one's life and the world. Not only the violations will appear, but also the repudiation of their validity and the confusion of their meaning for life in the world today. Like Paul we are living in times when our behavior baffles us.

Christlikeness is in the minority. Its value as well as its practicability have been lost sight of. This generation desires more to be like other men than like Christ. "What more are you doing than others?" (Matt. 5:47) is not a popular question.

The debate about the meanings of Christian ethics and morality in the more complicated aspects of modern life has excluded their consideration in the simpler and more personal relationships people have with one another. The starting point in applying the Christian morality to life has changed from first steps to the final ones. One would never think of teaching a child stair climbing by starting him at the top of the stairs. Yet in the application of Christian morals and ethics most of our teaching is just as unrealistic as that. Instead of teaching a person to begin with it where he can and go with it as far as he can, the modern attitude plunges him into a discussion of moot questions and complicated situations in the field of human conduct until he becomes so confused that he cannot take the simplest steps in Christian moral and ethical actions.

Christlikeness as a workable relationship faces serious misgivings in the midst of present world conditions. How can a person really live and act like a Christian today, surrounded by such universal unchristian practices in personal, social, economic, and political life, is more than an academic question. Every young person is conscious of it, and adults are being made cynical by the thought of it. Nevertheless, Christian teaching has practical advice to give to those who would make their everyday life worthy of the gospel of Christ. It points a way out through Jesus Christ. In obedience to him, Paul says, you are on your way to real living. And it must find a way to get the ear of this age. A perspective of history as well as a simplifying of the application of Christian morality to life will help to restore these lines of conduct to the Christian imprint. Hebrew and early Christian history supply the proof that Christlikeness is possible regardless of the circumstances. In a study of these peoples this age amid conditions similar to theirs sees how it can be done, which is a significant reason for the proper teaching of religious history in the public schools. Later events likewise testify to the practicability of the Christian demands upon life and the inevitability of the rewards which follow, thus exploding the theory that the unusual life-transforming power of the first century expended itself by the end of the third century and therefore its repetition is not to be expected in the twentieth century. The Quakers are a good example of how Christian conduct, understood and practiced, can win over the most unlikely conditions. Hardly more than three centuries ago they were a hated people, persecuted and discriminated against because of their way of life. They were faced with the alternatives of compromising and conforming to the prevailing customs or of holding fast to their ways. They held fast but with a purpose to win others to a recognition of the truth and to a respect for their way, and they won. Today the Quakers are the most universally trusted and respected group among the Christian denominations.

Such examples really supply the hope for the survival of the Christian imprint on conduct in an age when jungle ethics are creeping into the very heart of modern civilization. They teach that survival depends upon the strength of the inner man to stand fast. They point this generation to the way whereby a full life in Christ can be sustained. It lies in the path of Christian teaching in Christian discipline, a prescription offered by Paul to overcome the "beasts at Ephesus" (I Cor. 15:32). It centers in the individual. It wins by a sturdiness which nothing can weaken and a source of renewal which no environmental forces can quench. Christlikeness is a personal ideal. It never appears without an awakening within to the realization that above all else Christlikeness is one's supreme ambition. Then it is possible in spite of the most severe handicaps because human nature is so constituted as to be able to achieve the kind of personality

135

it sets its heart upon. Looking at a child in our midst and thinking of this tremendous fact about the molding of his future should, therefore, make a great difference in one's relationship to that child. Looking likewise on a world of people enticed to mold their personalities after the images of false gods, the challenge to the Christian influences to change man's model by the quickening of his deepest desires should take on the proportions of a new crusade.

Christlikeness, human conduct controlled and directed by the morality and ethics of Christ, is a creation of the mind and heart and will. It requires thought, feeling, and purpose to develop in its fullness. The way of its achievement as well as the evidences by which it is known constitute an aspect of education which must begin in the home and carry over into the molding social experiences beyond the home.

Loyalty in Paul's teaching supplied another distinguishing mark of the Christian imprint. The Christian is a man for Christ. Here again the term "loyalty" needs a Christian interpretation to be useful in Christian teaching. What is popularly thought of as loyalty and the considerations which motivate it will not supply the quality of life which maintains a Christian imprint in spite of everything. Loyalty for personal advantage is a contamination of the world which Christian nurture is constantly confronted with. Commitment up to a point is easy to secure for the Christian way of life; but unless it goes all the way, it is not sufficient either to produce or to maintain life on the Christian level. Secondary loyalties which bind life to good things but stand in the way of allegiance to the best are likewise deterrents to a clear and true Christian imprint upon life. The loyalty of approval is too easily substituted for the loyalty of support.

The quality of the loyalty required to make the Christian way the expression of one's life provides a large section in the teaching of Jesus. Some of the Master's standards sound severe, but none of them is superfluous. There is no cheap method for producing the Christian image. A restudy of the Christian meaning of loyalty in the light of decisions which modern life demands from the individual is a prerequisite for all who would make life over after the pattern of Christ.

The Christian image is sustained by the ultimates in loyalty. That is the demand because nothing less can develop the life. This is the significance of Jesus' comments about forsaking even family loyalties when they conflict with loyalty to him. It is the point of his parables, such as the one concerning the pearl of great price. It is the lesson in the episode of the rich young ruler who missed the best in life by a commendable but blind devotion to the second best.

Paul taught the subject of Christian loyalty with clarity and conviction because he could speak of it in terms of his own life. He bore in his body the marks of Christ and kept them bright and sharp by the loyalties which prevented any contamination by worldly erosions. His teaching on the subject also suggests an effective methodology for a modern approach. It could well be called the shock treatment because it was graphic, radical, and extreme. By it, however, Paul got attention for the subject and compelled a consideration of its full demands upon life. The implications of that loyalty run as a thread through all of Paul's letters to the churches. Live without limit for God, he writes to the Romans. People may ridicule you, he tells the Corinthians, but be willing to be considered a fool for Christ. Take the world's condemnation as an expression of Christ's commendation. You are ambassadors for Christ, he writes at another time, an office of highest trust and of complete devotion. Consider what that means in terms of loyalty. The world looks down upon you. It smirks at your cleanness, and it calls you names originally intended for derision, such as "Christians" or "Methodists" or "Quakers" or "Christers." Test your loyalty by how much you esteem "abuse suffered for the Christ" (Heb. 11:26).

Loyalty is no easy virtue. It can have no place in an effortless life. It will never appear in a curriculum of education through self-advancement. Often it is a bitter and costly experience. But here again Paul offers us an example of good teaching by explaining the demands of effort in terms of the joy of achievement. To Timothy, his special concern as a son in the ministry, he does not hide the hardship of the Christian life. "Indeed," he says, "all who desire to live a godly life in Christ Jesus will be persecuted." (II Tim. 3:12.) But that should not deter you from continuing "in what you have learned and have firmly believed, knowing from whom you learned it and how from childhood you have been acquainted with the sacred writings which are able to instruct you for salvation through faith in Christ Jesus, ... that the man of God may be complete. ... If we endure, we shall also reign with him." (II Tim. 3:14-15, 17; 2:12.)

Loyalty, however, is an ingredient of life which does best only when it is planted in its proper sequence. It cannot be applied as a finishing touch and be expected to deepen. The dominant loyalties of one's life are established early. Wise teachers select them carefully knowing their power to mark life for good or ill. And with equal care they make them a part of the developing life they seek to influence. Psychologists have discovered important information about the relationship of these early loyalties to later life. Their power is clearly established. Unworthy loyalties, fixed in the young, warp life. Worthy loyalties keep the development of life beautiful, healthy, and good.

Thus the time for molding into life the loyalties which will later stamp it is no longer debatable. They appear early. They are an experience which begins in childhood. How carefully they should be watched both for the right kind and for a good start! Self-centered loyalties grow and mar, and so often they are unwittingly nurtured by an unintelligent parental love. Tragedy awaits the life whose guiding and molding teachers have no worthy loyalties to place at its heart. It can never experience the strength and joy of a worthy attachment bigger and finer than itself. However, the allegiance to the best gets an early start in life also and, once firmly fixed, though it may become covered and submerged, is never eradicated. Its lines go deep into personality. This fact about the persistence of loyalties makes a starting point for the work of reclamation and restoration in lives where the imprint of Christ has been defaced. It is also a warning and an assurance to all who would influence and fashion lives for the best.

Following the example of Paul, it is the teacher's business to make converts who shall be faithful and loyal to him. (Rom. 1.)

Paul also called attention to the fact that the genuineness of the Christian imprint could be recognized by the quality of life which it attracted to itself. He held that identification could be determined by association and that its authenticity was shown by what adhered to it. Fellowship was his fourth distinctive mark of the stamp of Christ upon life. The finished work, he declared, will be a man with Christ. "Linked with Christ" was the phrase Paul used to describe this identifying relationship. And in his letters to the churches he referred to it as the shared life.

Perhaps this is the most difficult of all the marks of Christian identification to maintain, since the conditions under which we live make for loneliness and spiritual isolation rather than for fellowship. Reducing God to an intellectual concept which acknowledges his existence but denies his person has shut him out of the intimate fellowship which Christ promised. Many find Voltaire's description of his relation to God that "he saluted but did not speak" more congenial to their life and thinking than David Livingstone's assurance that, since Christ was a gentleman, he would keep his promise to be with his children always. Consequently a sense of spiritual loneliness and irresponsibility, paradoxically enough, are the manifestations of an age of religious belief.

While the twentieth century has done much to tear down the social and racial barriers which have separated the human race and inhibited their sharing a fellowship with Christ, it has at the same time witnessed the erection of political and intellectual barriers which have made the practical expression of fellowship on a universal scale nearly impossible. A billion people are now living under political systems which discourage the fellowship of Christ within and restrict it with those on the outside. These two factors in modern life have combined to produce a neurosis of loneliness which has reached epidemic proportions. They are responsible for a large number of the world's peculiar people. Cut off from a sense of Christ's presence within and denied the expressions of that Christian fellowship in their contacts with others, the view of life becomes distorted and the conduct of life becomes unnatural. The fear of loneliness which has destroyed the healing and strengthening exercise of meditation shows up in the demand for continual excitement, noise, lights, and sleeping pills. It has produced an age of outwardly normal but inwardly antisocial people. Their thoughts are evil toward one another. They are consumed by an inner rage against the actions of their fellow man. They drop to low levels of thought, to enslaving habits of conduct, and to anti-Christian attitudes. Many who suffer from the effects of this sense of isolation are religious people at least in name and in church membership. They believe in God and Christ, but there is a blank spot in their belief which actually takes God out of their daily lives. They accept the Christ of yesterday, the Jesus of history, and they believe in the Christ of tomorrow who will eventually reign in the world, but they have no experience of a personal relationship to Christ now. They do not feel his "presence every passing hour." Near though he may be, our generation, like the Emmaus travelers, has not been trained to recognize him in the common daily experiences of life. Its social education on the side of the spirit has been bungled.

Now the reasons for this blind spot in man's spiritual-social relations which deny him a sense of vital fellowship with the spirit of Christ goes back to the beginnings of the education which should lead to a mature man in Christ. Sensitivity to the spiritual in later years depends upon the nurture and development of its presence in the young. Every child has it; and until the artificialities of living start choking it out, this sense of the closeness of God to his children is a very beautiful and natural experience. How often mature people long for the strength of the simple acceptance of God, which was real to them once but which has vanished because of either neglect or mistreatment. And how stupid to ridicule the simplicity and reality of a child-like faith when Jesus made it the open door to the kingdom of Heaven. For, says William Blake,

> He who mocks the infant's faith
> Shall be mocked in age and death.

EDUCATION AS GUARDIAN AND GUARANTOR

Education, Christian and secular, in the home, church, school, or community, is the guardian of that heritage, its conservator and its developer. Education brightens and deepens or dims and confuses spiritual sensitivity. The attitude it encourages, the intellectual atmosphere it creates, the marks of maturity it strives for, all affect the quality and reality of man's spiritual relationships. Education has a responsibility for maintaining a simple faith in a complicated life, a consciousness of divine direction in a world of tangled human relations, a comradeship with spiritual life amid the loneliness of material accumulations. When the busy and successful, by the world's standards, think of it, this is really what they would wish for their children—something which vanished from their life and for the loss of which nothing they have created themselves can compensate.

How education in all its phases can keep alive and growing this sense of the closeness and the communicability of God yields to no pat formula. It is more likely accomplished as a by-product of the total educational impact. All that happens in all the places and by all the people, whose lives leave an impress upon other lives, affects the quality of the Christian fellowship in its outward and upward relations. The child begins with the glowing reality of the fact, and his education should guard it from the tarnishing doubts which a pseudo self-sufficiency and an absorbing interest in things create. The history of its loss is generally a story of competing concerns which "filch away man's time for fellowship with God." Education in its widest application has both a responsibility and an opportunity to keep this relationship in the forefront of the values it inculcates.

Often the closeness of this human-spiritual friendship is determined by the word man takes for authority in his life. Is it to be the word of God verified by experience, or is it to be the opinions of men based on limited knowledge and inadequate experience? The tests for some sure word about the nature and extent of the divine-human relationship have not been interpreted to modern youth as Eli took time to do for the young Samuel or as Susannah Wesley made it her business to do in the education of her children. Left to the hit-or-miss methods of chance, many come to maturity with no adequate tests for the reality of spiritual experiences, only to discover that they have let slip out of their lives the one element which gives endurance and purpose to all other achievements. When the educational forces look upon the child committed to their molding powers and ask, "What is to be the [child's] manner of life?" (Judg. 13:12), the future of his spiritual perception and his ability to develop spiritual contacts becomes a determining consideration in the answer.

Finally, education through all its contributing agencies has a responsibility not only to create the Christian imprint, but to set it. The work of creating is futile unless the image is so firmly fixed that the conditions of living regardless of what they are will strengthen it and not wear it away. Its failure to stand up is the area of greatest loss in Christian living.

Here again education must accept its destiny and be judged by the outcome. To this end was it born, and for this cause it came into the world. The Greeks recognized the test of true education to be the endurance of a good imprint. "By education," Plato said in his *Laws*, "we mean that training in virtue from youth up that makes a man passionately desire to become a perfect citizen, knowing how to rule and obey with justice. The properly educated become good." The Judaic-Christian hope rested in a society educated to know the way of righteousness and by proper training and personal equipment to be able to stand up under life's deteriorating pressures.

Therefore, it is necessary not only to create the stamp and superscription of Christ upon human life, but also to make sure that the image does not wear away when circulated in modern society. A debasement of the currency of Christian personality is the strategy now in use to destroy the Christian way of life. It retains the form but reduces its value. The likeness of Christian culture and morality are recognizable, but their character is foreign to their Christian pretensions. The institutions of Christianity are continued, but their Christian products are inferior. They speak the words which give life, but their ring from the heart lacks genuineness. Their imprint is conventional and not natural. It is superimposed by custom but is unsupported by principle and intellectual belief. Its form is easily marred because of the metal of life on which it is impressed. Therein lies the danger to a realization of a truly Christian social order and to the maturing of persons to the fullness of Christ. The vital element which guarantees permanence can be dropped out and not really missed until it has wreaked havoc.

Slight alterations have been taking place in the evidences of the Christian life around the world. In accepting them we are prone to say that they need not seriously affect the quality or the power of the Christian world order or of the individual exercise of a life, in, for, like, and with Christ. But always such changes in moral outlook, divine allegiance, and Christian conduct have debased and cheapened life. They have stood in the way of the establishing of the kingdom of God on earth and of the attainment of the abundant life within it. This oft-repeated strategy of evil is the present danger to life at its best in our day. And while we are waiting to change these conditions, we must strengthen the individual's inner powers to resist their effect if we are to avert these personal life-destroying tragedies which are multiplying with alarming rapidity.

Just as a doctor gives a patient a regimen to live by after the cure is complete and the gymnast outlines the exercises which will keep the body strong and fit, so the Christian parent, teacher, and citizen cannot leave the Christian lives they have molded without some final instruction for their continuance and improvement.

What fixes the Christian imprint so that it endures and emerges in spite of everything?

When we bear in mind that the nonspecialist in the home and community, as well as the specialist in the church and school, will be engaged in what may be called the servicing of the finished work for permanence and effectiveness, suggestions for this fixing process should be within the ability of all to perform. With this requirement in mind let us consider three.

First, to keep the imprint true to its original, there must be the sustaining power of the right example. Out of sight is soon to be out of mind. And memory is not the most trustworthy faculty for preserving the accuracy of detail. So those who dealt with this problem in its first necessity, the New Testament writers, saw the need of keeping the vision of goodness vivid if the life of goodness was to be kept true to it. They bid the Christian to fix his thoughts on Jesus, to keep Christ in mind. To be changed to his likeness, they said, one must gaze "with unveiled face, beholding the glory of the Lord" (II Cor. 3:18).

Paul had much to say about the necessity of clear vision and the constancy of high aim. If one is looking for a list of practical exercises to keep before him the vision of the best, he will find it in Paul's letters to the early Christians. Not only the principles are to be found in them, but the specific exercises as well. These are the things you should aim at, Paul says. Not eating and drinking—pagans make that their aim. But doing right, making peace, finding joy in what God does—in building yourselves and one another up in these, he tells the Romans, should be your aim. (Rom. 14:17-23.) Aim at something higher and better than yourselves. Imitate the Christlike virtues; make love your aim, Paul writes to the Corinthian Christians. Always aim at what is kind to one another and all the world, he tells the Christians in Thessalonica; aim at integrity and to satisfy your commanders, he counsels Timothy, his son in the gospel.

The educational soundness of these admonitions has been reiterated by wise men in every walk of life. We borrow our behavior from what we see most of. Shakespeare pointed to the source of greatness in the power of a good example (King John). And contemporary educators, such as Whitehead, testify to the released powers of education through maintaining the "enduring vision of goodness."

What our children see most of and what our associates think most about are strong forces at work upon the character lines of their own being. This being the case, there is small wonder that juvenile delinquency is increasing and adults do not realize what manner of persons they have become.

Paul's second suggestion for maintaining the Christian imprint is the correcting power of a Christian discipline. To the Corinthians he said, "You should be looking at yourselves to make sure that you are really Christ's" (II Cor. 13:5 Phillips). Self-examination is one of the most difficult and deceptive of all the intellectual and spiritual exercises. How easy it is to idolize our image in a mirror and to see in ourselves the look we desire but which does not exist.

Discipline has faced ostracism in modern life. The cult of mediocrity has removed a sense of the need for discipline. The ordinary person can be a drifter. He may indulge himself. For him life may appear as a picnic. But the price he pays is high and deceiving because it is not all collected at once. He doesn't realize that he can never stop paying when he replaces his aim for perfection with an accommodation to the common run of life. Social popularity has brought more than one prodigal son to the pigsty of personal degeneracy.

It was the discovery of this fact about preserving life at its best which maintained Greek life at its best for seven hundred years after its most serious threat of annihilation. The Greek philosophers, such as Socrates and Heraclitus, at a time when the environmental forces were threatening the Greek standards of life, turned the searchlight of truth within. "Know thyself," they said; "search thyself" and you will find the breaches which give the enemy entrance and the power also which can push back the enemies to your way of life.

How like our present day! Discipline having gone out of life, the enemies of the best have taken over. Its departure has cut the nerve of high attainment, not only in the personal conduct of life, where the godly example is acknowledged and ignored; but also in the intellectual attainments of the present, where both art and ideas fall short of their historic examples. Modern painting, music, craftsmanship, and philosophy excel in creating for themselves fads but fail to survive the age which popularized them.

Pure religion also suffers from a lack of discipline. The size of church giving and church membership should be showing greater evidence in Christian living. But the dividends have not grown commensurately with the assets. And the causes for this underproductivity point to a removal of the strengthening disciplines which characterized the Church in the age of its amazing greatness. It is this careless participation which is the reason for the many feeble and weak Christians in the Church today. (I Cor. 11.)

So we face the need for constant checking and rechecking, the comparison of the standard with the performance, and the exercise of discipline for achievement if the Christian imprint is to emerge as the popular pattern of life. For only when we examine ourselves beforehand can we avoid the judgments of God. (I Cor. 11:31 Phillips.)

The widely criticized conduct of modern life will show no improvement and losses to an inferior way will continue unless and until a re-establishment of discipline in all phases of human growth is accepted as normal and necessary rather than traditional and therefore antiquated.

The third suggestion for confirming the Christian imprint in life is the creating power of cross-fertilization, the checking of theory by experience, the adjustment of the past to the present, the verification of an idea by the manner in which it works. The Christian way of life could never have taken root in the society of the first century if its exponents had not based its validity on the practical realities of its claim. Jesus set the pattern by inviting people to come and see, then go and do. The early Christians found Christ before they wrote about him. They possessed the changed life before they described it. Paul with his penchant for abstractions based his theology not on thought alone but on ideas verified by experience.

Theories of life can be the subject of endless argument, but a demonstration in living is final for the individual. In the popular mind a theory is true only if it works.

The deterioration of the Christian imprint, its fading and dimming, can be fully explained only by the current challenge to traditional belief. The argument that just because our fathers believed in this morality is no undebatable reason for their children living by it finds some plausibility in the tremendous changes which have taken place in scientific thought. The revolt is largely a repudiation of theory, and the Christian forces are losing the battle because they are fighting it on the field of argument rather than on the surer ground of experience. We submit the Christian way of life to a people for judgment who have had no experience with it on which to base a judgment. Furthermore, we do them harm by encouraging them to believe that without an experience with it themselves or a knowledge of the experience of others with it they are competent to judge. It seems ridiculous to argue about Christianity with a person who knows nothing about the Bible, but we do. In no other field of knowledge and decision, such as medicine or chemistry, would we think of debating with an ignoramus. Thus the authority of the Bible is repudiated by people who know nothing of its content, and Christian morality is rejected by people who have had no experience with it. The prejudice which stands in the way of Christianity's good standing is not by any means all on the side of its proponents. The most blatant bigotry and prejudice often appear in the arrogance of those who reject Christianity without acquiring any personal knowledge of it.

Therefore the Christian educator must do most of his teaching in the laboratory of life and in the field trips of past history and of current observation. Whether he is a parent, a professional teacher, or a responsible citizen, his task and responsibility are to prevent the rejection of the good life solely on theory and logic. The intangible factors do not appear in a syllogism, but they are important for a right decision. And the good life is kept on the highest plane of effectiveness when the word is matched with the deed and when men's questions are taken to the experience of living for the answers.

Just as a picture is worth ten thousand words, so one consistently good life can silence the doubts of an inquiring age in revolt against tradition.

Christian education has that person both in the original and in reproductions. The Christian imprint is best because in life it works out best. And all of us as molders of others can look with assurance to the permanence of our handiwork if its value can be seen in us.

INDEX

Livingstone, David, 139
Livingstone, Sir Richard, 24, 120
Loneliness, 139, 140
Lot, 86
Love, 96, 123
Loyalty, 136, 137, 138, 139
Lucifer, 17

Man, 99
  in Christ, 130, 136
  Christian doctrine of, 118
  value of, 118
Manoah, 36, 37, 39, 44, 100
Martha, 126
Mary, mother of Jesus, 30, 110, 111
Mary, sister of Martha, 126
Materialism, 14. *See also* Secularism
Maturity, individual, 40
McKenney, Ruth, 51
Meaning of life, 113
Mediocrity, 146
Meditation, 140
Methodists, 137
Methods of education, 60, 69, 109, 125
Mind, Christian doctrine of the, 101-9
Ministry, 48, 49
Modern life, 146
Molding forces, 28-34
Molding purpose, 58-61
Money, 41
Moral imperatives, 77, 78
Moral neutralism, 78
Moral patriotism, 79
Moral platitudes, 95
Moral purpose, 77
Moral relativism, 22
Moral responsibilities, 123
Morality, 60, 98, 108. *See also* Morals
Morality, Christian, 101, 133, 134, 136, 143, 148
Morals, 59, 96, 99, 100, 101. *See also* Morality
Morrison, Charles Clayton, 102
Moses, 54
Motivation, 100, 101, 113

Motive of action, 118
Music, 49

Naboth, 12
Naturalism, 95, 100. *See also* Materialism *and* Secularism
Nebuchadnezzar, 86
Neutrality in religion, 48
New Testament, 96, 144. *See also* Bible
Nichols, James H., 45

Objective, 122
Optimism, 66
Overconfidence, 123
Overemphasis, 66
Overenthusiasm, 66

Pain, 41
Parents, 44, 46, 52, 54, 85, 89, 109, 114, 122, 127, 128, 148
Patriotism, false, 22
Paul, 54, 57, 61, 70, 92, 96, 97, 99, 100, 112, 122, 128, 129, 130, 131, 132, 133, 134, 135, 136, 137, 138, 139, 145, 147
Perfection, 146
Personal interest, 125
Personality, 13, 31, 34, 135, 136
  Christian, 124, 143
  public school as molder of, 30
Pessimism, 74
Peter, 57, 126
Phelps, William Lyon, 34
Phillips, J. B., 97
Philosophers
  Christian, 103
  Greek, 146
Philosophy
  of Christian education, 123
  of education, 80
  of life, 45, 83, 92, 93, 102, 118, 127
  modern, 146
Plato, 14, 15, 77, 92, 143
Political crisis, 133